REASON AND RIGHT

14.95

Reason and Right

GARTH HALLETT

UNIVERSITY OF NOTRE DAME PRESS
NOTRE DAME, INDIANA 46556

Copyright © 1984 by
University of Notre Dame Press
Notre Dame, Indiana 46556
All Rights Reserved

Library of Congress Cataloging in Publication Data

Hallett, Garth.
　Reason and right.

　Includes bibliographical references and index.
　1. Ethics. 2. Social ethics. I. Title.
BJ1012.H24　1984　　170　　83-40595
ISBN 0-268-01621-6
ISBN 0-268-01622-4 (pbk.)

Manufactured in the United States of America

Contents

PREFACE	ix
PART ONE: THE THEORY AND PRACTICE OF MORAL REASONING	1
CHAPTER 1: MORAL REASONING	3
A Survey of Moral Reasoning	3
(1) THOUGHTS	4
(2) REASONING	7
(3) MORAL REASONING	10
How Much Moral Reasoning Should We Do?	19
FRAMEWORK QUESTIONS	21
ETHICAL FRAMEWORK QUESTIONS	24
ETHICS, THE STUDY OF FRAMEWORK QUESTIONS	26
CHAPTER 2: ARE ANSWERS POSSIBLE?	31
Grounds of Moral Skepticism	33
THE FIRST GROUND: DISAGREEMENT	34
THE SECOND GROUND: INTRACTABILITY	37
SUMMING UP	39
Sources of the Impression	39
A FIRST SOURCE OF THE IMPRESSION: DIFFICULTY	40
A SECOND SOURCE: TIED VERDICTS	44
A THIRD SOURCE: EMOTIONAL INVOLVEMENT	47
Practical Implications	49
CHAPTER 3: SOUND MORAL ARGUMENTS	53
Moral Arguments	53
Patterns of Argument	55
Real-Life Arguments	60

Contents

The Strength of Arguments	68
Evaluating Arguments	69
A Standard Procedure	72
From the Argument into the Issue	76

CHAPTER 4: ANALYSIS AND CHARITY— TWIN INSTRUMENTS OF TRUTH — 79

The Principle of Charity	80
Illustrations	81
A Fatal Configuration	85
Arguments for Analysis	90
1. SELLING HOMEWORK	91
2. ORGAN TRANSPLANTS	91
3. A-BOMBING	91
4. LYING	92
5. ABORTION	92
6. SMOKING	93
7. ARTIFICIAL CONTRACEPTION	93
8. SUICIDE	93
9. EXTRAMARITAL SEX	94

PART TWO: ARGUMENTS AND ISSUES — 97

CHAPTER 5: RIVAL APPROACHES — 99

Arguments for Analysis and Evaluation	99
1. TRUMAN'S DECISION TO USE THE ATOMIC BOMB	99
2. HIROSHIMA AND NAGASAKI	100
3. EUTHANASIA	101
4. WARFARE	101
5. SELF-DEFENSE	102
6. CONTRACEPTION	102
7. HELPFULNESS	102
8. TRUTHFULNESS	103
Background Remarks	103
A SAMPLE DERIVATION	105
NOT JUST CONSEQUENCES	106
APPLICATION	107
A SAMPLE CONFRONTATION	109
OTHER RIVALS	110
Further Reading	111
Sample Analysis-Evaluation: #5 (Self-Defense)	112

CHAPTER 6: UNIVERSAL NORMS — 114
Arguments for Analysis and Evaluation — 114
1. ADULTERY — 114
2. WAR — 115
3. ABORTION — 115
4. INFORMED CONSENT — 116
5. SMOKING — 116
6. FAMILY HEAD — 117
7. DIVORCE — 118
8. CONFIDENTIALITY — 119

Background Remarks — 119
(1) ANALYTIC OR SYNTHETIC — 121
(2) POSITIVE OR NEGATIVE — 123
(3) SUMMARY OR SUPPLEMENTARY — 125
(4) ACTUAL OR POSSIBLE — 126
SUMMING UP — 128

Further Reading — 129
Sample Analysis-Evaluation: #7 (Divorce) — 129

CHAPTER 7: RULES OF PREFERENCE — 132
Arguments for Analysis and Evaluation — 132
1. AIDING THE NEEDY — 132
2. HONESTY IN BUSINESS — 134
3. GRAFT — 135
4. FREER TRADE — 135
5. IMMIGRATION — 136
6. DYING THAT OTHERS MAY LIVE — 136
7. GUARANTEED ANNUAL INCOME — 137
8. FOR FOREIGN AID — 138
9. AGAINST FOREIGN AID — 138

Background Remarks — 138
Further Reading — 145
Sample Analysis-Evaluation: #5 (Immigration) — 146

CHAPTER 8: MORALITY AND LAW — 148
A. *Legislation* — 148
Arguments for Analysis and Evaluation — 148
1. LEGALIZING HARD DRUGS — 148
2. SEAT BELTS — 149
3. ABORTION — 149
4. PROSTITUTION — 150

5. EUTHANASIA	150
6. NUDISM	151
7. PORNOGRAPHY	151
8. MARIHUANA	152
Background Remarks	152
MILL'S RULE	153
MILL'S GROUNDS	154
ALTERNATIVE GUIDELINES	155
Further Reading	157
Sample Evaluation, of a Law from Argument 1	158
B. *Obedience*	160
Arguments for Analysis and Evaluation	160
1. CHARITY VERSUS THE LAW	160
2. CAR THEFT	160
3. PAYING TAXES	161
4. ABORTION	161
5. ILLEGAL DEMONSTRATIONS	162
6. STUDENT SIT-INS	163
7. PROTESTING INJUSTICE	164
8. SYMBOLIC DISOBEDIENCE	164
Background Remarks	165
Further Reading	171
Sample Evaluation, Applying the Three Conditions to Argument 8	171
RETROSPECT	175
APPENDIX A: FURTHER ARGUMENTS AND ISSUES	178
Arguments for Analysis and Evaluation	178
1. PRISONS	178
2. ANIMALS' RIGHTS	179
3. REVERSE DISCRIMINATION	180
4. NUCLEAR FREEZE	181
5. POLICE AND FIREFIGHTERS' STRIKES	181
6. DEMOCRATIZING MANAGEMENT	182
7. EDUCATION	182
8. CAPITAL PUNISHMENT	183
9. HOMOSEXUALITY	183
10. PARENTS AND CHILDREN	183
APPENDIX B: VALUE-BALANCING	185
NOTES	187

Preface

The popular text of a friend of mine bears the title *Right and Reason*. I have kept the same words, since they fit the present work equally well, but have reversed their order, to suggest a shift in emphasis and structure, reflecting a different rationale.

An introductory course in ethics should, I believe, do three main things:
  (1) discuss specific moral problems,
  (2) acquaint with background theory, and
  (3) train in moral reasoning.
Most ethics texts stress the first two and slight or omit the third. Yet mere discussion of problems and/or theory, without instruction and practice in ethical reasoning, seems an inadequate answer to life's needs. It does not prepare students to handle on their own the many issues they will encounter not covered by the course's limited sampling.

This text opens, therefore, with a four-chapter introduction, first to ethics and moral reasoning generally (chapters 1 and 2), then to the analysis, evaluation, and conduct of moral reasoning (chapters 3 and 4). The remaining four chapters, with numerous sample arguments to choose from, then provides much practice in such analysis, evaluation, and personal reflection on specific moral problems — far more, indeed, than most courses will have time for. Background remarks, bearing directly on the arguments and issues of each chapter, add a theoretical dimension to the discussion. In this coherent fashion all three components in turn — reasoning, problems, and theory — receive their due.

Instructors who wish to include training in moral reasoning but to emphasize it less may omit the second half of chapter 4, so as to arrive more quickly at the problems and theory of part two, or may bypass the chapter entirely and introduce the Principle of Charity as occasion suggests — say in exercise 4 of chapter 3. (See the Teacher's Guide.)

I am grateful to Gerald Cavanagh, Thomas Schubeck, and the anonymous readers of University of Notre Dame Press for valuable comments. Further suggestions for improvement will be welcome. They can reach me at the Department of Philosophy, University of Detroit, Detroit, MI 48221.

PART ONE

The Theory and Practice of Moral Reasoning

For most people moral reasoning is, I imagine, a rather mysterious activity. Though it is something they do often, perhaps daily, if asked to characterize it even roughly, they would be at a loss for words. Though they repeatedly search for moral answers, and debate them strenuously, at the same time they harbor notions which, if true, would seem to make answers impossible and debate futile. Though they attach great importance to the solutions arrived at, they attend little to the process by which they are reached or to its soundness. If, then, there is truth in Socrates' saying that "The unexamined life is not worth living," it would seem that moral reasoning—so momentous yet so little understood—is a good place to start looking closely at our lives.

It is, however, just a place to start, not a place to end or to linger too long. The chapters of this first part of the book deal at some length with the questions just cited: the nature and need of moral reasoning (chapter 1), its validity and possibility (chapter 2), norms and procedures for assessing its soundness (chapters 3 and 4). Yet from the beginning concrete moral arguments and issues are also present, first as illustrations, then as samples for analysis and evaluation, and, finally, at the end of chapter 4, as much for themselves as for purposes of illustration. Once part one has prepared the way, emphasis can shift from theory to practice. In part two the reflection Socrates urged will extend to all areas of life: marriage, welfare, business, drugs, sex, research, taxes, demonstrations, smoking, honesty, foreign aid, immigration, law and order, war and peace. . . . Appendix A adds still other topics.

CHAPTER 1

Moral Reasoning

In an oft-quoted passage of Molière's *Le bourgeois gentilhomme* M. Jourdain inquires: "What? When I say, 'Nicole, bring me my slippers, and give me my nightcap,' that's prose?" Assured it is, he exclaims in wonder: "Gracious me! I've been talking prose for the last forty years and never knew it." Some might react the same way were they told they had been doing moral reasoning all their lives. At the age of three, when Jeff got the bigger piece, they argued it wasn't fair. Somewhat later, when they found a wallet in the park, they reflected earnestly what they should do with it. Still later, when they joined the debate team, they lined up reasons for and against each practical position they debated. But no one told them, then or earlier, that what they were doing was "moral reasoning."

The chances are good that it was. It might be something of an exaggeration, though, to say we've engaged in moral reasoning "all our lives." Much of our thinking doesn't merit the label "reasoning." Much of it doesn't concern moral matters. And even when it does, the reasoning we go through may not be moral reasoning. So as a matter of fact, our moral reasoning is rather spotty and sporadic. Whether it should be as brief and infrequent as it is is a question we will want to consider. But first let's get a clearer picture of the facts, as best we can.

A SURVEY OF MORAL REASONING

Just how much reasoning people do, as distinct from other forms of thought, and how much moral reasoning they do, as distinct from other forms of reasoning, is difficult to determine. Consider, for instance, the following episode:

> One fall evening several years ago a young woman, Kitty Genovese, was attacked, robbed and stabbed on a street in Kew Gardens, N.Y. When her assailant came upon her she began to scream and resist. The man struggled with her, and finally stabbed her leaving her bleeding on the sidewalk. She dragged herself several yards into the doorway of a nearby building, all the while moaning and calling loudly for help. The whole process took several minutes. Later the police determined that a total of 38 people heard the screams or actually viewed the event from the windows of their apartments. No one did anything to help, not even call the police, and the woman subsequently died.[1]

Here we are given the outer drama, the account of what did, and did not, happen that evening in the street. But what took place inside, unseen? What feelings and thoughts and possible reasonings passed through the minds of those 38 people? Concerning that inner, decisive drama — or rather those 38 interior dramas enacted concurrently in the witnesses roundabout — we possess only fragmentary evidence. Still, though our data are meager, there will be profit in asking and attempting to answer the following three questions, in order: (1) Is it likely that *any thoughts* of assisting her passed through those people's minds? (2) If they did, were the thoughts *reasoning*? (3) If so, were they *moral* reasoning?

(1) Thoughts

The first question may look easy. Surely they all *thought* of helping. After all, here was a fellow human being, being stabbed to death. It isn't as though they heard a faucet dripping, or a phone ringing, or a bus passing by in the street. The woman screamed for help. They knew that something horrible was happening to her. How could they escape the thought that perhaps they should do something about it?

Well, consider the somewhat similar situation mentioned by an argument in chapter 7 that follows: "Though we do not see the famine-stricken people of India and Africa and South America, we can never quite forget that they are there. Now and then their faces are shown in the news, or in the begging ads of mission and relief organizations." We know they are out there. We know they are in dire, mortal need. But do we give them a thought, or does the ad or appeal simply register as an ad or appeal for the needy in this or that place, and then we pass on? Is it really all that certain, in this case, that everyone thus *seeing* or *hearing*, as those 38 did in Kew Gardens, also becomes an involved, *thinking* witness of what he or she sees or hears?

We have good reason to doubt it, don't we? In fact we may know better from our own experience. We're on a federal loan, say, wondering when and how we'll repay it, so don't consider for an instant whether we should feed people in Calcutta. Or maybe we have children to support. Or we've adopted a set policy, of giving so much to the United Fund, so much to the church, and that's it. Or we're saving to buy a color TV. Or . . . In countless ways — some good, some bad, some debatable — our minds may be fixed in advance, so that "seeing we do not see, and hearing we do not hear." The ad, the appeal, the picture of starving people registers briefly, and we pass on, without a thought that perhaps we are the ones who should help.

Sometimes, too, the voice of the needy is muted. Take for instance the case of a Wall Street secretary, in another argument of chapter 7. She knows that her boss has decided to manipulate the price of a stock. She also knows — she could tell you if you asked her — that when stocks are manipulated, lots of little investors are likely to get hurt.

Maybe ruined. She knows they're out there, somewhere, but she doesn't see them or hear them or know who they are. So she may not give them a thought. After all, "it happens every day."

A stabbing, though, especially a noisy, public stabbing, does not happen every day. And those 38 people did see or hear the woman in distress. Is it likely, then, that hearing her screams or actually viewing the assault, they did not give at least a fleeting thought to the possibility of helping her? Could anyone be that callous, that inhuman? Reading the results of subsequent inquiries, one wonders.

> One couple, now willing to talk about that night, said they heard the first screams. The husband looked thoughtfully at the bookstore where the killer first grabbed Miss Genovese.
>
> "We went to the window to see what was happening," he said, "but the light from our bedroom made it difficult to see the street." The wife, still apprehensive, added: "I put out the light and we were able to see better."
>
> Asked why they hadn't called the police, she shrugged and replied: "I don't know."[2]

Could she honestly answer "I don't know" if she had given the matter any thought that night or had discussed it with her husband?

Yet others apparently did at least *consider* doing something. "A housewife, knowingly if quite casual, said, 'We thought it was a lover's quarrel.' A husband and wife both said, 'Frankly, we were afraid.' They seemed aware of the fact that events might have been different. A distraught woman, wiping her hands in her apron, said, 'I didn't want my husband to get involved.'"[3] Others may have thought: "It's too dangerous," "Someone else will do something," "I have no weapon," "There are hundreds of people on this block," "I'm not strong enough to help," "If I go out there, it means trouble, complications," "I can't go out in my shorts," "If he's stabbing her he might stab me," "It'll be all over before I get there," "Maybe it's not as bad as she makes it sound," "Someone should help, but why me?" Articulate or half-formed, such are the thoughts we can imagine slipping through the consciousness of most of the 38.

We sense they weren't enough. Surely we would have done more, we think. Yet the reactions of 38 people, in a respectable neighborhood, may tell us something about ourselves as well as about them. Doubtless we too might be more open than we are, more perceptive of others and their needs, more alive to the appeals, muted or screamed, that reach us, more or less frequently, more or less clearly, according as we are tuned to receive them. That is one function of an ethics course. Through examples and discussions it jogs the moral imagination. It says "Look here!" "Pay attention!" "Should you really close your eyes and ears that way?" "Is your reason a good one?"

(2) Reasoning

With the varied likely reasons and reflections of the majority before us, we can now ask: Were they *reasoning*? This is not as idle a question as it may at first appear. For we shall do a lot of reasoning here, and the very word "reasoning" turns some people off. So let's get a clearer notion of just what reasoning is, and how it differs, for instance, from mere thinking.

An example of mere thinking would be M. Jourdain's "Gracious me! I've been talking prose for the last forty years and never knew it." That's a thought, but not yet reasoning. Again, if an apprehensive resident reflected, "I wonder if my door is locked," that too would be a thought, but not reasoning. Typically, reasoning has a purpose, a direction. It looks for an answer. Thus the knowing housewife quoted above may have reasoned if she first wondered what was happening, then thought of some possibilities, and finally concluded that it was probably a lover's quarrel.

8 Moral Reasoning

What, though, of the episodic bits we imagined in the minds of other witnesses? Would the mere thought "It's too dangerous" be reasoning? Why might we be inclined to say it is? Well, *what* is too dangerous? Going out and helping her. So that thought has preceded this one and is being answered. The words are a response. Unpack them, and we

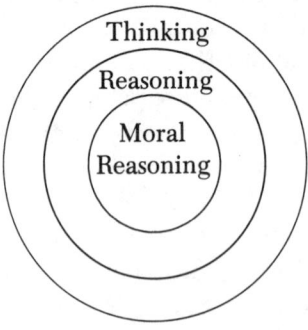

discover a beginning ("Should I?" "Shall I?"), a middle ("too dangerous"), and an end ("No, I won't," "No, I shouldn't"). And much the same might be said for every item in the list. Each of the thoughts we have imagined is answering, implicitly, the question: "Shall I, should I, help?" Each has a direction. So we could say that all these people did at least some rudimentary reasoning.

Viewed one way, this reasoning looks good. At least it shows some minimal concern. The appeal has registered. It is sensed, if only dimly, as addressed to them. A question has stuck in their minds, and now they are answering it. Without the question there would be no reasoning, but only random thoughts. Only "I wonder if my door is locked" or "A lively place, this Kew Gardens." When contrasted thus with unconcern or with unconcern for others, this reasoning, revealing at least incipient involvement, looks commendable.

But not, of course, when it is contrasted with effective action. Then all these excuses appear worse than worthless. And how fertile the human psyche is in such rationalizations! That's what gives reasoning a bad name. We imagine people safely indoors, debating with themselves whether to help, whether they are the ones who should do it, whether they're really obliged to — and all the while Kitty Genovese is getting stabbed to death in the street. And yet it is fairly obvious, if we reflect a little farther, that the fault is not with reasoning as such but with this particular reasoning.

For suppose people were willing and eager to help. Determining the best way might call for some hasty reasoning. "Should I put some clothes on first or go as I am?" "Should I go this instant or find a weapon?" "Should I do what I can or call the police?" This is all rational reflection and gives reasoning no bad name.

We might say that only such reasoning is true to itself — true to its nature as reasoning and not just thought — whereas the rationalizing kind is not. For as we saw, reasoning typically has a direction: it seeks an answer; whereas when conscience whispers "Shouldn't you help?" and we look for excuses, we're not so much trying to answer the question as to quiet the questioner. If conscience spoke too audibly, too insistently, there might be hell to pay. Kitty might have company in the morgue.

Still, sham reasoning or genuine, it's all called reasoning. And there is no arguing with usage. So we won't reserve the name "reasoning" for the good kind and deny it to rationalizations. But we shall emphasize the difference. That is what ethics does. It keeps us honest. It deftly nets our reflections on the wing and holds them up for inspection — closer inspection, perhaps, than we find comfortable. We squirm a little on the pin, and wish our thoughts could flutter more freely and naturally again.

Are we really sincere in our reasoning, or only fooling ourselves? Do we genuinely desire an answer, or are we just putting off an inner or outer questioner? An ethics course — at least one like the present — carries this query further. If you really want solutions, it suggests, then reason well, for that is the surest way to find them. And if you want to reason well, then learn what effective reasoning looks like. Acquire some expertise at this lifelong, all-purpose activity. In this way, too, ethics keeps us honest.

(3) Moral Reasoning

Appropriate instruction may help with our moral inquiries. But what kind are they? What counts as a *moral* question? Were the people we have imagined that evening, with their varied thoughts, asking and answering moral questions? And was their reasoning therefore *moral* reasoning? This third query in our list of three will permit us to get a clearer picture not only of the frequency of specifically moral reasoning, as opposed to other varieties, but also of ethics and its role.

We are all familiar with moral statements, employing terms like "right" and "wrong," "should" and "shouldn't"; but we may not have observed what is distinctive about them. We may not have noticed, for example, that they are categorical, not conditional, and so apply to everyone, regardless of personal preferences.

When I say they are *"categorical,"* I have the following difference in mind. Suppose someone advises, "If you want to get ahead, work hard." That is a conditional statement. If you want to succeed, do this; if you don't — well, that is up to you. Moral statements, however, are more decisive. The moral "should" in "You *should* support your parents," for example, leaves no room for contrary preferences. It rules out the proviso "unless, that is, you would rather take life easy, or spend the extra cash on yourself." Again, if a person declares "Torture is wrong," this does not generally mean "You should refrain from torture unless, perhaps, it gives you pleasure or proves convenient." You should not, period. A moral "should" or "shouldn't" is categorical, not conditional. And therefore it speaks to all.

Thus even when moral statements concern a single

individual—you or me or Jim Skladany—they are implicitly universal in a way that other statements are not. When, for instance, someone says "I *want* to do so-and-so" or "I *shall* do so-and-so," there is no suggestion that other people want the same thing or intend to act the same way. The speaker speaks for his or her self alone. When, however, a person asserts morally "I *should* do so-and-so," the implication is that anybody in relevantly similar circumstances should do likewise. And whoever says "You *shouldn't* have done it" implies that he or she, if similarly placed, shouldn't have done it either. Such is the logic of moral terms like "should" and "shouldn't" and of moral discourse generally.

In confirmation of this analysis, imagine a dialog like the following: "Marge, you shouldn't have told on Alice." "Why not? *You* did." "I know, but that was different." "How was it different?" At this point the original speaker had better come up with some relevant difference between her situation and Marge's, or else she will be forced to admit either that she too did wrong *or* that Marge did no wrong. Like obligation in like circumstances: such is the logic of *moral* judgments.

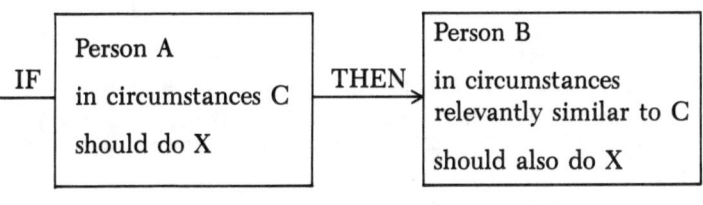

Along the sidelines, however, as Kitty was getting stabbed, people may have been thinking principally of Number One. If they asked themselves "Shall I?" it may have meant not "Should I?" but simply "What is safest, most convenient, most prudent for me? What is in *my* best interests?" And in that case the thought "I'm not dressed" or "I might get hurt" would be a prudential calculation, not a specimen of moral reasoning.

True, people might conceivably calculate prudentially and still be reasoning morally. For there is such a thing as *ethical* egoism. Self-interest may rate as a moral theory if a person is ready to say: "The very best way for *all* of us to live is for each to look out for himself. That may mean being kind to others in the expectation that I will thereby advance my own ends. But in a crunch, when Kitty's in the street and I'm safe inside, I may judge it more prudent — and therefore more moral — to stay where I am." To this explanation, however, the egoist, if ethical, would have to add: "And if ever the tables are turned and I need your help, you'll be doing the right thing if you turn a deaf ear to my screams." And it may be doubted whether many people would be willing to append this rider. Egoists may be common, but sincere ethical egoists are doubtless a much rarer breed.

But how common are egoists? We need to know if we are to estimate the frequency of moral reasoning, as opposed to self-serving calculations. So we are obliged to attend, if only in passing, to the doctrine known as *psychological egoism*. According to this view, once common in philosophy and still widely current in psychology and popular thought, we are all of us egoistic in all we do. For whatever we desire and seek, whatever we hope and strive for, is something that, if achieved or attained, is likely to gratify us. It is our own satisfaction, then, that forever leads us on.

Were this doctrine true, it might appear to simplify greatly our inquiry into the frequency of moral reasoning. For such reasoning, we noted, looks beyond sheer self-interest: it considers what *all* should do in similar circumstances. So if we are all of us self-seeking, always and everywhere and in all we do, it might seem that there is never any genuine moral reasoning, on that occasion in Kew Gardens or on any other.

Egoism and Altruism	
Psychological egoism "All acts are basically selfish."	*Psychological altruism* "Some acts are basically unselfish."
Ethical egoism "You should look out only for yourself."	*Ethical altruism* "You should look out also (or only) for others."

This doctrine of psychological egoism, however, seems quite certainly mistaken. Whatever we desire, it says, we desire solely as a means to our own happiness. Yet is that why one person has his heart set on finding a cure for cancer, another aspires to fame, another seeks justice for the Gypsies, another works for world socialism, another collects coins, another saves up for a posh villa, and so on through the infinitely varied objects of human desire? Is each indifferent to the specific goal save as it promises to bring him or her some pleasure? Isn't it clearly the other way around, the pleasure resulting from the fact that what we have attained is the very thing we longed for? Satisfaction, we might say, is the shadow cast by satisfied desires — desires of other things than satisfaction.

The point appears with special clarity in an incident recounted of Abraham Lincoln. Though in reality one of the most altruistic of people,

> Lincoln once remarked to a fellow-passenger on an old-time mud-coach that all men were prompted by selfishness in doing good. His fellow-passenger was antagonizing this position when they were passing over a corduroy bridge that spanned a slough. As they crossed this bridge they espied an old razor-backed sow on the bank making a terrible noise because her pigs had got into the slough and were in danger of

drowning. As the old coach began to climb the hill, Mr. Lincoln called out, "Driver, can't you stop just a moment?" Then Mr. Lincoln jumped out, ran back, and lifted the little pigs out of the mud and water and placed them on the bank. When he returned, his companion remarked: "Now, Abe, where does selfishness come in on this little episode?" "Why, bless your soul, Ed, that was the very essence of selfishness. I should have had no peace of mind all day had I gone on and left that suffering old sow worrying over those pigs. I did it to get peace of mind, don't you see?"[4]

To this explanation Lincoln's companion might have replied: "But tell me, Abe, why did the sow's suffering cause you more distress than it did the rest of us? Why did you get any satisfaction from helping her? Why didn't you find pleasure and peace of mind by clubbing her over the head and chopping her piglets in pieces? Why wouldn't that have warmed your heart all day, rather than getting yourself wet and sloppy pulling them out of the slough?" The answer, of course, would be that Lincoln was concerned for the pigs, and not just for Abraham Lincoln. To call his action basically selfish was to get things turned around. His concern for the pig and her piglets explained his satisfaction in helping them; his prospective satisfaction did not explain his concern.

And yet there is plenty of selfishness in the world. That is, there are plenty of people who find their satisfaction in amassing wealth for themselves, fame for themselves, power for themselves, pleasure for themselves, and so forth, and attend very little to the needs and desires of other people (let alone pigs), whereas there are those who derive genuine satisfaction from creating a better life for their fellow human beings, and perhaps have their hearts set on that more than on personal gain. And something of the same mixture is to be found in all of us, with egoism or altruism more or less ascendant, habitually or at any given moment. So how about the witnesses and their reasoning?

How many, shall we say, reasoned morally? How many looked out for themselves? How many tried to do both (answering conscience's query, but in a self-serving manner)?

No statistical estimate seems possible. So the reader can sense once again why I warned that the facts are hard to come by and proposed to survey them "as best we can." Here too, though, our inquiry suggests a possible benefit of studying ethics. There are those who, when asked to consider the pros and cons of a given line of action, automatically translate the request into "What's in it for me?" The pros and cons they mention, for even a social issue, are all personal advantages and disadvantages. Ethics, however, opens a broader perspective. Familiarizing us with the moral point of view as distinct from narrow self-interest, it thereby reveals an alternative we may not have considered seriously. The choice is ours. Ethics will not make it for us. But at least the option and the challenge are made clear: the natural selfishness with which we are born versus the moral viewpoint of which we are also capable. One or the other.

Let us look back now and take stock. To the three questions concerning our sample episode we have reached the following answers: (1) Most of the 38 probably did consider helping Kitty; (2) their thoughts were probably reasoning; (3) but it is difficult to judge how many reasoned morally, how many merely prudentially. The full difficulty of an estimate concerning the frequency of moral reasoning appears when we consider that this is but a single case, and not particularly typical. Here the issue was thrust on people's attention, so that they could hardly ignore it. Other times it is not. A bloated child stares silently from the pages of a magazine. Victims of a stock manipulation hover vaguely out of view, neither heard nor seen. The goose force-fed to produce the foie gras on a gourmet's plate impinges on practically no one's consciousness. Out of sight out of mind. Only the farmer adverts to the cruel cramming.

Reviewing these varied occasions for moral reflection

and our varied responses to them, we arrive back where we began, but see more clearly now why and to what extent it might be an exaggeration to say we have engaged in moral reasoning "all our lives." "Off and on, and oftener off than on, most of our lives" would be a more careful, if stodgy, assessment. For, many occasions for moral reasoning elicit none from us (think of the foie gras on our plate). Much of our thinking is not reasoning ("Poor goose," the farmer perhaps reflects, then rams more down its throat). Much of it doesn't concern moral matters (the housewife surmises what is happening in the street). And even when it does, the reasoning we engage in may not be moral reasoning (we perhaps puzzle "What's best for me?" rather than "What should I do?"). So, as I said before, our moral reasoning is rather spotty and sporadic. Whether it should be as brief and infrequent as it is is the question we shall now consider.

EXERCISE 1

1. (Review) How much moral reasoning, if any, can you detect in the following passages? That is, in which can you detect *reasoning*, meant to determine what *ought* to be done, in the strong, moral sense of "ought"? (You need not agree with the reasoning or its conclusion to classify it as "moral," any more than you need agree with historical reasoning to call it historical, or with scientific reasoning to call it scientific. As there may be bad historical or scientific reasoning, so there may be bad moral reasoning.)

a. "'Meggie, sometimes things just don't happen the way you want them to. You ought to know that. We Clearys have been taught to work together for the good of all, never to think of ourselves first. But I don't agree with that; I think we ought to be able to think of ourselves first. I want to go away because I'm seventeen and it's time I made a life for myself. But Daddy says no, I'm needed at home for the good of the family as a whole. And because I'm not twenty-one, I've got to do as Daddy says.'

"Meggie nodded earnestly, trying to untangle the threads of Frank's explanation."
(From Colleen McCullough's novel, *The Thorn Birds*)

b. "She invoked the Sermon on the Mount in order to persuade people, especially 'the old crowd' with which she had grown up, to accept changes that meant higher taxes and fewer luxuries. If the country did just the temporary and expedient things 'we will find ourselves again just where we are today, still building a civilization on human suffering.'"
(Joseph Lash, on Eleanor Roosevelt, in *Eleanor and Franklin*)

c. "Muhammad Ali, commenting on his choice of career: 'I once thought about playing football. But you have to wear too much equipment and people can't see you.'"
("Personal Glimpses," *Reader's Digest*, May 1981)

d. "Because prostitution is private sexual conduct between consenting adults, the state should not proscribe it unless the state can demonstrate that it involves substantial harmful public consequences."
(George F. Will, in *The Washington Post*, August 26, 1974)

e. "The steward said to himself, 'What am I to do now that my employer is dismissing me? I am not strong enough to dig, and too proud to beg. I know what I must do, to make sure that, when I have to leave, there will be people to give me house and home.' He summoned his master's debtors one by one. To the first he said, 'How much do you owe my master?' He replied, 'A thousand gallons of olive oil.' He said, 'Here is your account. Sit down and make it five hundred; and be quick about it.' Then he said to another, 'And you, how much do you owe?' He said, 'A thousand bushels of wheat,' and was told, 'Take your account and make it eight hundred.'"
(Luke 16:3–7)

f. "By virtue of the nature of modern weapons and the situation prevailing on our planet, even when motivated by a concern for legitimate defense, the armaments race is, in fact, a danger, an injustice, a mistake, a sin and a folly."
(Vatican declaration, 1976)

g. "In some cases the best design is no design, as with a love letter, which is simply an outpouring, or with a casual essay, which is a ramble. But in most cases, planning must be a deliberate prelude to writing. The first principle of composition, therefore, is to foresee or determine the shape of what is to come and pursue that shape."
(William Strunk, Jr., and E. B. White, *The Elements of Style*)

h. "On the average, Britons save 13% of their disposable income. West Germans save 15%. Japanese, 26%. But Americans save only 4.5%!

"A major reason people in other nations save more is that they are given tax incentives by their governments.

"The U.S. actually *discourages* savings, by taxing the interest that is earned.

"Isn't it time Congress gave savers a *real* tax incentive? We think the annual tax-free limit on savings interest should be raised to $1,000 for individuals and $2,000 for joint tax returns."
(Advertisement of The Savings and Loan Foundation, Inc., in *National Geographic Magazine*, March 1981).

2. (Review and Preparation) How much moral reasoning do you think typically goes into decisions of the following sorts, and why?

a. mapping the final move in a tied basketball game

b. daily exercise

c. planning a counterattack

d. voting for a presidential candidate

e. deciding to read a book

f. swimming to the rescue of a person attacked by a shark

g. organizing a party

h. choosing a career

HOW MUCH MORAL REASONING SHOULD WE DO?

"Should moral reasoning be as brief and infrequent as it is?" The question is an important one, for life and for a course in ethics. If moral deliberation should be frequent or at least prolonged, a text like this, with its stress on moral reasoning, makes good sense. If, on the contrary, there is relatively little need of moral reasoning, the need for such a text and such a course is correspondingly slight. And serious suggestions have in fact been advanced which might appear to carry this implication.

In a talk to teachers the pragmatist philosopher William James declared for instance:

> Ninety-nine hundredths or, possibly, nine hundred and ninety-nine thousandths of our activity is purely automatic and habitual, from our rising in the morning to our lying down each night. Our dressing and undressing, our eating and drinking, our greetings and partings, our hat-raisings and giving way for ladies to precede, nay, even most of the forms of our common speech, are things of a type so fixed by repetition as almost to be classed as reflex actions. To each sort of impression we have an automatic, ready-made response.[5]

In James's view this is not only how things are but also how they should be. "The great thing in all education," he continues,

> is to *make our nervous system our ally instead of our enemy.* It is to fund and capitalize our acquisitions, and live at ease upon the interest of the fund. *For this we must make automatic and habitual, as early as possible, as many useful actions as we can,* and as carefully guard against the growing into ways that are likely to be disadvantageous. The more of the details of our daily life we can hand over to the effortless

custody of automatism, the more our higher powers of mind will be set free for their own proper work. There is no more miserable human being than one in whom nothing is habitual but indecision, and for whom the lighting of every cigar, the drinking of every cup, the time of rising and going to bed every day, and the beginning of every bit of work are subjects of express volitional deliberation. Full half the time of such a man goes to the deciding or regretting of matters which ought to be so ingrained in him as practically not to exist for his consciousness at all. If there be such daily duties not yet ingrained in any of my hearers, let him begin this very hour to set the matter right.

Here is a recommendation worth considering. What percentage of our conduct should thus be rendered routine? Eighty? Ninety? Ninety-nine point nine? Whatever the precise verdict we reach—I'll not debate the matter here—there is much to be said for James's line of thought. Yet it would seem, overall, to reduce moral deliberation. The more questions are settled in advance, the less reflecting we shall need to do, ethical or other. Only rarely will a stabbing in the street or the like intrude on the steady, tranquil flow of our lives, calling for decision and perhaps deliberation. Moral reasoning, it may appear, can be saved for special occasions.

Yet even were the occasions as rare as this picture suggests, the importance of moral reasoning would not thereby be lessened. For the more numerous the acts fixed by initial decisions, the more consequential those decisions would be, and the more deserving of careful scrutiny. Those who live from moment to moment need not think very long or hard whether to smoke *this* cigar, rise *this* morning ten minutes later, dine *this* evening at eight, and so forth. But once the decision being made concerns all future smoking, all future rising, all future dining, or the like, it becomes momentous, and we had better give it our best reflection. Let James multiply such resolutions as he pleases: every restriction on the number of decisions we make heightens proportionately the significance of those that remain, and longer deliberations should therefore replace the more frequent. Hence the appropriate quantity of moral reflection, overall, may remain much the same.

Framework Questions

Despite his initial illustrations, of rising, dressing, greeting, drinking, and the like, James had something more than just "daily duties" in mind; a different sort of decision comes into view when he quotes from Charles Darwin's autobiography. "Up to the age of thirty, or beyond it," wrote the great scientist,

> poetry of many kinds, such as the works of Milton, Gray, Byron, Wordsworth, Coleridge, and Shelley, gave me great pleasure, and even as a schoolboy I took intense delight in Shakespeare, especially in the historical plays. I have also said that formerly pictures gave me considerable, and music very great delight. But now for many years I cannot endure to read a line of poetry; I have tried lately to read Shakespeare, and found it so intolerably dull that it nauseated me. I have also almost lost my taste for pictures or music. . . . My mind seems to have become a kind of machine for grinding general laws out of large collections of facts, but why this should have caused the atrophy of that part of the brain alone, on which the higher tastes depend, I cannot conceive. . . . If I had to live my life again, I would have made a rule to read some poetry and listen to some music at least once every week; for perhaps the parts of my brain now atrophied would thus have been kept alive through use. The loss of these tastes is a loss of happiness, and may possi-

bly be injurious to the intellect, and more probably to the moral character, by enfeebling the emotional part of our nature.[6]

The proposed rule, "to read some poetry and listen to some music at least once every week," illustrates a new type of decision. James's earlier examples we might describe as "repetition decisions," whereas the new variety we might call "framework decisions." In the first kind the actions adopted are practically invariant: one brushes one's teeth, ties one's shoes, fixes breakfast, drives to school, lights a cigarette, greets friends, rises and goes to bed in much the same fashion time after time, day after day. In the second type of option, on the contrary, there is much variation, and the decision just indicates the direction, or provides the general setting for future, more particular decisions. Hence the name "framework decision." For within the same picture frame, say, one may fit paintings, photos, lithographs, sketches, woodcuts, or etchings, of the most varied contents and styles: still lifes, portraits, or battle scenes; oils, pastels, ink, tempera, or watercolors; realist, impressionist, cubist, surrealist, or abstract. So too within the general rule to read some poetry and listen to some music Darwin might have fitted lyrics, ballads, psalms, sonnets, epics, or odes; operas, operettas, concertos, symphonies, sonatas, polyphony, lieder, or madrigals; of varied content and style, read or heard on different occasions, in different settings, for varying lengths of time. While fixing a general framework, the decision would allow much leeway, and doubtless Darwin would use it. He would not read the same poem every week of his life, or listen to the selfsame piece of music, as he might use the same razor or smoke the same brand of cigarettes.

Most of our lives' more consequential options belong to this second category. When, for example, we decide upon a job, career, hobby, spouse, house, school, party, religion, church, child, adoption, fraternity, partner, research topic, or academic major, a framework is fixed within which we then work out myriad details while disregarding endless possibilities that lie outside the frame. Having taken a secretarial position, for instance, with a given firm, we type letters, take dictation, file documents, answer phone calls, take a coffee break, and so forth, in a pattern that varies each day. Yet each morning we head to one particular office, deal with one familiar set of people there, and perform a specific range of tasks, while giving no thought to countless other work places, work companions, and conceivable duties that alternative choices would have brought with them. Our decision is not irrevocable, to be sure, but while it lasts it provides a general focus for our lives.

From what has been said it is clear that each such decision greatly reduces our "express volitional deliberation" in the manner James recommended. We would never get on with being a doctor, or with our medical studies, say, if we kept on debating, day after day, whether it might not be better to teach or preach or go into cancer research. It is equally clear, however, that such framework decisions do not diminish the importance, or perhaps even the desirable overall amount, of moral deliberation. For one thing, many particulars remain to be determined within each focus. For another, the options being so consequential, they deserve more careful consideration; the process of decision, though not repeated, should at least be prolonged.

Thus a quasi-mathematical relation can be stated for framework decisions as for repetition decisions. If we follow James's recommendation, we shall make fewer decisions, but each decision will cover more actions, so will be more important, so will merit lengthier reflection. If we ignore his advice and adopt a piecemeal approach to life, we shall make more numerous decisions, but each decision will cover fewer actions, so will be less important, so will deserve less attention. In one case fewer decisions but lengthier; in the other more decisions but shorter: in either alternative the desirable amount of deliberation may remain much the same.

Ethical Framework Questions

You may be wondering, though, what all this has to do with *moral* reasoning. Would Darwin's decision be a *moral* decision? Would it settle a moral issue and result in a *moral* rule? And would the reflection that went into it therefore be moral reasoning? Do people reason morally when, as I just suggested, they "decide upon a job, career, hobby, spouse, house, school, party, religion, church, child, adoption, fraternity, partner, research topic, or academic major"? Granted, these are important options, but are they ethical?

Yes, such consequential choices are as ethical as any others. If it makes sense to ask "Should I?" and not just "Shall I?" about a lie, an abortion, a homicide, or extramarital sex, it makes equally good sense to ask the same question about a career, a marriage, an academic major, a lifelong use of free time. The latter questions may be as momentous as the former, may merit like consideration, and may receive replies that are just as categorical and universal, in the sense we have seen, as more typically "moral" queries. A person may decide, upon deliberation, that he or she *should* marry, *should* take up a hobby, *should* move south, *should* not run for office, and so forth. And the "should," each time, may be unqualified, so carry the implication that anyone, similarly placed, should do likewise.

This assessment runs counter, I know, to a common impression that only certain matters are moral, others not. Surely it is not a *moral* question, you may feel inclined to object, whether, for example, I save up and buy a motorcycle, learn to play the guitar, or turn to gardening as a hobby? Surely there is no right or wrong to a choice like that?

Well, what in general, would you say, makes an action right or wrong? What is the test of morality? Most people would agree that right and wrong relate somehow to the happiness and welfare of human beings. If I can save a person from drowning, a child from snakebite, a neighborhood from urban blight, a country from war, I should do so. I should do that good, prevent that harm. And the same test applies to lesser options like those just mentioned. Buying a motorcycle, learning to play the guitar, and taking up gardening as a hobby may not be life-or-death decisions, but they do have implications for human happiness and therefore have moral relevance.

Suppose, for example, that I am thinking of growing a garden. The time and money I spend on the project, both of which may be considerable, are time and money I might spend otherwise, for myself or others. If I grow flowers, they may add color to the neighborhood, decorate my livingroom, ornament a Mardi Gras float, or brighten up the office. If I grow vegetables, I may eat them myself, sell them for profit, share them with relatives and friends, or donate them to a local food center. So the decision matters; it matters morally.

> "To exist as a man means to act. And action means choosing, deciding. What is the right choice? What ought I to do? What ought we to do? This is the question before which every man is objectively placed. And whatever may be the results of his examination of the question as a question, it is the question to which he never ceases for a moment objectively to give an answer." *Karl Barth*

Practically any standard of right and wrong currently in use would yield the same verdict. Whether one defines morality in terms of happiness and welfare, as above, or in terms of naturalness, or divine will, or love, or universalizability, or respect for persons (some alternatives from chapter 5), the decision for or against gardening will qualify as a moral decision. It will satisfy or violate the general norm and therefore will be right or wrong.

Ethics, the Study of Framework Questions

If general principles are so important for individual choices, they too deserve careful scrutiny. That is the business of ethics. It focuses on the broad moral frameworks within which our actions and decisions fall. Thus you will not find in a book of ethics any discussion of Peter's promise or Susy's abortion or company X's merger, anymore than you will discover a discussion of the Smith's cat in a biology text or of Ted's kite in a book of physics. What you will find instead are general norms to guide such particular choices. Some of the norms concern specific categories of actions (e.g., promises, abortions, and business transactions). Others, like the duty to obey God or follow nature or promote human welfare, are still more general, covering all areas of behavior. They state standards that any action should satisfy.

The broader the framework option, the wiser James's advice appears, to decide early, well, and once for all. His recommendation applies, if anything, with greater force to an all-inclusive standard of conduct than it does, say, to a rule for employing one's leisure time. Darwin, it is true, should not have let things drift; by taking thought too late about literature, music, and art he missed a chance for extra happiness and a more fully human existence. However, the outcome might have been more tragic had he given as little consideration to still broader options and had he recognized at the end, through experience or fuller reflection, that he had ruined the whole of his life and not just part of it.

An ethics course offers an occasion to think out life's biggest questions, in time, and to match the length of reflection to the largeness of the issues. "How much moral reasoning should we do?" we asked at the start of this section. None, I would say, before brushing one's teeth or the like. Some, no doubt, when, for instance, we decide for life whether to brush every day. More for consequential framework decisions like Darwin's. Still more, the same logic would suggest, when the questions are broader yet and decisive for more actions. A full semester of study and reflection may then not be enough.

EXERCISE 2

1. Though no sharp line divides one category from the other, which of the following would you classify as repetition decisions, which as framework decisions, which as neither?

   a. the choice of a course

   b. the choice of a vacation spot

   c. the choice of food in the cafeteria line

   d. the decision to do a good deed each day

   e. the decision to use an electric razor

   f. the decision to stop and help a stranded motorist

   g. the decision to take up sewing as a hobby

   h. the decision to grow a beard

   i. the decision to write one's congressman

   j. the decision to enlist in the Navy

   k. the decision to take the bus each day rather than drive to school

2. Concretely and still more fully than in the chapter's illustrations (Darwin, the secretary), spell out the implications

of some specific personal framework decision (a specific career, academic major, marriage, research project, sorority, church affiliation, . . .), indicating in how many different ways and how varied it would affect a person's life, within the limits set. How many choices would have to be made that otherwise would not arise?

3. Comment on the quantity and quality of Darwin's moral reflection at this turning point in his life (the decision was later reversed, thanks to his uncle's decisive intervention):

"He then learned from his father and sisters that a letter (which they appear to have read) had arrived from Professor Henslow. Enclosed with it was another letter from George Peacock, a Cambridge mathematician and astronomer who was responsible for nominating naturalists to naval ships making surveys; in it he made that completely unexpected offer to young Darwin of the post of unpaid naturalist aboard HMS *Beagle*. Here was a bolt from the blue. He had never thought of himself as a serious naturalist, a professional naturalist, or indeed eligible for any scientific job; he was to be a clergyman. Then again this bizarre proposition cut so drastically across his plans; after the partridge shooting he had hoped to make a journey down to the Canary Islands before taking holy orders. And yet — why not? He was inclined to accept. Henslow, who had recommended him to Peacock, was most pressing that he should. . . .

"Dr Darwin [Charles' father] had other views. He thought it was a wild scheme; Charles had already switched from medicine and now he was running away from the Church; he was not used to the sea and would be away for two years or more; he would be uncomfortable; he would never settle down after he got back; he would harm his reputation as a serious clergyman; others must have been offered the post before him, and since they had refused there must be something fishy about it; in short, a useless undertaking.

"Dr Darwin did not absolutely forbid Charles to accept the appointment, but he made himself emphatic. 'If,' he said, 'you can find any man of common sense who advises you to go I will give my consent.'

"Charles was in no position to argue. His allowance (which he had overspent at Cambridge) was his only source of income, and although subconsciously he may have wanted to get away from his father he would never have dreamed of defying his authority. Reluctantly he wrote to Henslow saying that he could not go."

(Alan Moorehead, *Darwin and the Beagle*)

4. The diagram below shows a set of framework options ranging from broader to narrower, with each narrower decision arrived at within a broader framework. Draw a diagram or two of your own showing similar sets of possible options, one within the other.

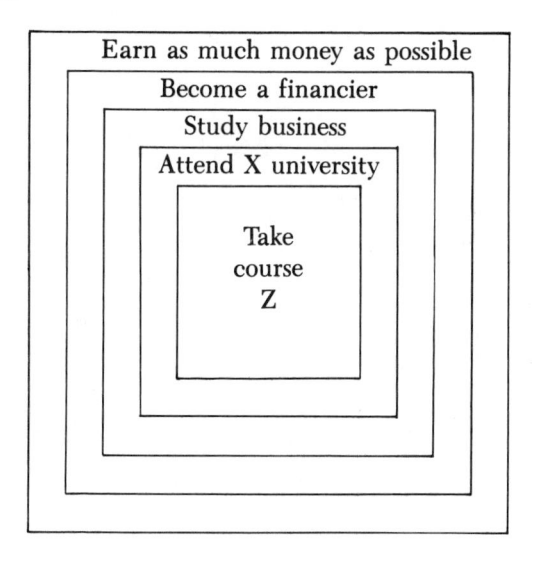

```
┌─────────────────────────────────────┐
│    Earn as much money as possible   │
│  ┌───────────────────────────────┐  │
│  │      Become a financier       │  │
│  │  ┌─────────────────────────┐  │  │
│  │  │     Study business      │  │  │
│  │  │  ┌───────────────────┐  │  │  │
│  │  │  │ Attend X university│  │  │  │
│  │  │  │                   │  │  │  │
│  │  │  │       Take        │  │  │  │
│  │  │  │      course       │  │  │  │
│  │  │  │        Z          │  │  │  │
│  │  │  │                   │  │  │  │
│  │  │  └───────────────────┘  │  │  │
│  │  └─────────────────────────┘  │  │
│  └───────────────────────────────┘  │
└─────────────────────────────────────┘
```

5. To review the whole chapter, answer the following questions:

   a. How does reasoning typically differ from mere thought?

   b. How does moral reasoning differ from nonmoral?

30 Moral Reasoning

   c. Distinguish between the doctrine of ethical egoism and that of psychological egoism.

   d. Why is ethical egoism rare?

   e. Why does psychological egoism seem mistaken?

   f. How do framework decisions differ from repetition decisions?

   g. Why does neither kind clearly lessen the desirable amount of moral reasoning?

   h. Why are important decisions all equally moral in character?

   i. How do the framework questions studied in ethics differ, say, from Darwin's?

   j. Why, therefore, would they seem to merit still more reflection than his?

CHAPTER 2

Are Answers Possible?

Robert E. Lee fought for the Southern cause in the Civil War, sincerely. Abraham Lincoln opposed it, sincerely. And both were intelligent men. So who was right? Such a disagreement might create the impression that there are no right answers to ethical questions, and that moral reasoning is therefore a delusion and a waste of time. The stakes may be high, and the issues many, as the last chapter maintained; so moral deliberation would be important if it led to truer solutions. But if one answer is as good as another — if a Lincoln and a Lee are equally correct — then we may as well flip a coin, or do as we please. We need not think long and hard about momentous issues, as conscientious people tend to do.

We need not trouble, for example, whether states' rights are prior to federal, or whether this nation "of the people, for the people, and by the people" shall and should survive. We may simply consider what side our friends are fighting on, or which is likelier to win. Or we may prefer to sit the conflict out, if we can, as much the safer course. And if our conscience starts to trouble us — if it suggests that we are "cowards" or "opportunists" — we may treat it too as a delusion, born of our upbringing and reflecting the mistaken assumption that some lines of action are better than others.

Such an attitude is not just a possibility but a widespread reality. Before moral reasoning can even get under way, or before it has proceeded very far, people are likely to object: "Who is to say what is right or wrong? Everyone has a right to his or her opinion." Lincoln has a right to his; Lee has a right to his. Who are we to dictate the one true answer?

"In my opinion," writes a reader of *Playboy Magazine*,

> to ask whether or not a given act, such as mate swapping, is moral is to pose a meaningless question. There are those who still believe that some supernatural monarch has decreed a code of rules by which we must live, but they are on ground only slightly less unsound than those who still reject evolution. Nor can any modern-minded atheist or agnostic prove, philosophically or scientifically, that any set of secular rules or obligations is superior to the individual's own desires. Modern ideologues may tell us we have a duty to humanity, society, reason or revolution till they are blue — or red — in the face, but they are human, like everyone else, and why should one man's code bind another?[1]

It is instructive to observe the author of this letter, Dion O'Glass, then argue that people should not feel bound by ethical codes — which "are but convenient (and, too often, inconvenient) fictions"— nor seek guidance in a higher rationale. "They need reassurance that there is something more important backing their decisions than their own feelings. But individual feelings are the most important thing there is. Religions, philosophies and ideologies are, in a sense, illusions: They have only such size and power as we assign them."

This argument is instructive, I say, because it does the very thing it ridicules. It declares what we should or should not do. It bases itself on an ideology or philosophy — one O'Glass fittingly labels "libertarian thought." And this ideology, with its claim that "individual feelings are the most important thing there is," has only such "size and power" as the writer of the letter assigns it. It is not backed by any stated reasons. The letter cites no grounds for accepting its general stance rather than any other.

The letter is instructive, furthermore, because this inner tension and apparent contradiction between what it says and what it does characterize much of our society. Many a person will declare at one moment that right and wrong are matters of personal preference, that one answer is as valid as another, and the next moment will be arguing strenuously for or against some position. If right and wrong were mere matters of taste, argument would be futile. If argument is appropriate, then some solutions must be better than others. Or so it would seem. And yet, as I say, the same ambivalence that appears in the *Playboy* letter is common in our culture as a whole.

Where, then, does the truth lie? Facing serious issues, often of life and death — capital punishment, aid to El Salvador, abortion, mercy killing, atomic arms — we hesitate to simply flip a coin. That seems somehow inappropriate. Yet if one answer is as good as another, and we have no personal preference, isn't it a perfectly rational way to make up our minds? You can sense, then, that this widespread impression that all answers are equally valid deserves closer examination, not only for the purposes of this book, but for the general coherence of our lives. How does the skeptical impression arise? What grounds, if any, does it rest on?

GROUNDS OF MORAL SKEPTICISM

"Most men," writes Bertrand Russell, "are inclined to agree with Hamlet: 'There is nothing good or bad but thinking makes it so.' It is supposed that ethical preferences are a mere matter of taste."[2] For this view Russell suggests two main grounds. It is rendered plausible, he says, "by the divergence of opinion as to what is good and bad, and by the difficulty of finding arguments to persuade people who differ from us in such a question."

Russell may be right about the tendency of most people to view good and bad, right and wrong, as mere matters of taste. They are not general skeptics. They do not deny that anything can be known. Many matters — of history, theology, mathematics, physics, or psychology — they treat as factual. But not ethical questions. Such questions, they believe, have no correct or preferable solutions, and therefore none can be discovered.

Russell may also be right about the grounds for this common view; people's reasons may be the ones he cites. Not that most people have thought about these matters or could suggest any grounds for their skeptical assumptions. Moral skepticism is something they pick up, unreflectively, like measles or depth vision. Yet I have found that when a student, say, succeeds in articulating a reason for the skeptical position so many students share, it invariably turns out to be one of the two in Russell's list. And it usually coincides with the first: people disagree on moral matters.

So let us weigh this reason (disagreement), then the other (difficulty of persuasion). If one or the other ground proves conclusive, the charge against moral knowledge will have been sustained; a sentence of "guilty as charged" will be warranted, and the search for ethical answers can cease. If, on the contrary, neither ground looks at all convincing, the charge against moral knowledge will have to be dropped until such time as sounder evidence is adduced. Moral skepticism will not have been refuted, nor will the existence of moral knowledge have been proved, any more than a defendant's innocence is proved by the collapse of the case brought against him. Important clues may have been overlooked. Still, as in a court trial, we shall be entitled to say, "Innocent until proven guilty," and to continue debating moral issues, on the assumption that some solutions are indeed preferable to others.

The First Ground: Disagreement

Striking instances of diversity in ethical views have long been known, and cultural anthropologists keep turning up new ones. Some years ago, for example, Ruth Benedict described a society in northwest Melanesia where no one might work with another and no one might share with another. "But there was one man of sunny, kindly disposition who liked work and liked to be helpful. The compulsion was too strong for him to repress it in favor of the opposite tendencies of his culture. Men and women never spoke of him without laughing; he was silly and simple and definitely crazy. Nevertheless, to the ethnologist used to a culture that has, in Christianity, made his type the model of all virtue, he seemed a pleasant fellow."[3]

Such antithetical attitudes as these—Christian, Melanesian, or other—do indeed suggest greater kinship with matters of taste than with judgments of objective fact. People differ this completely concerning the tastiness of turnips or the choice of school colors but not concerning the chemical composition of sugar or the sources of the Nile. However, as Renford Bambrough observes:

> The objection loses much of its plausibility as soon as we insist on comparing the comparable. We are usually invited to contrast our admirably close agreement that there is a glass of water on the table with the depth, vigour and tenacity of our disagreements about capital punishment, abortion, birth control and nuclear disarmament. But this is a game that may be played by two or more players. A sufficient reply in kind is to contrast our general agreement that this child [about to undergo painful surgery] should have an anaesthetic with the strength and warmth of the disagreements between cosmologists and radio astronomers about the interpretation of certain radio-astronomical observations. If the moral sceptic then reminds us of Christian Science we can offer him in exchange the Flat Earth Society.[4]

The earth has a specific shape. It is or isn't flat; it is or isn't spherical. Both answers are not equally accurate. Yet people have disagreed about the earth's shape, and still do. (I recall the tale of a friend of mine concerning the astonishment of an African student when he realized, finally, that the earth really *was* spherical.) And Bambrough could have cited many other questions on which there is more disagreement but to which there evidently are right and wrong answers. But this could not be if the argument for moral skepticism was valid. For the argument implies that the moment people disagree, the question they disagree on has no correct answer.

Bambrough's refutation seems amply confirmed, for example, by the instance Benedict cited. By her own account the Melanesians' factual views, underlying their moral code, diverged as spectacularly from our own. "In this tribe," she wrote,

> the exogamic groups look upon each other as prime manipulators of black magic, so that one marries always into an enemy group which remains for life one's deadly and unappeasable foes. They look upon a good garden crop as a confession of theft, for everyone is engaged in making magic to induce into his garden the productiveness of his neighbor's; therefore no secrecy in the island is so rigidly insisted upon as the secrecy of a man's harvesting of his yams. Their polite phrase at the acceptance of a gift is, "And if you now poison me, how shall I repay you this present?" Their preoccupation with poisoning is constant; no woman ever leaves her cooking pot for a moment unattended. Even the great affinal economic exchanges that are characteristic of this Melanesian culture area are quite altered in Dobu since they are incompatible with this fear and distrust that pervades the culture. . . . They go farther and people the whole world outside their own quarters with such malignant spirits that all-night feasts and ceremonials simply do not occur here. They have even religiously enforced customs that forbid the sharing of seed even in one fam-

ily group. Anyone else's food is deadly poison to you, so that communality of stores is out of the question.[5]

We disagree on these factual matters. We do not believe in black magic. We do not believe it affects productivity. We do not believe the world outside their quarters swarms with malignant spirits. We do not believe that the food of one is poison to the other. So are our beliefs no more accurate than theirs? Does our very disagreement prove there is no right or wrong answer to any of these questions? Surely not. So the first ground for moral skepticism — the mere fact of disagreement — is invalid.

The Second Ground: Intractability

Perhaps more influential in philosophical circles as an objection to moral knowledge is the second reason Russell cites: "the difficulty of finding arguments to persuade people who differ from us in such a question." If a person thinks parsnips delicious and I find them repulsive, what more can I say? How could I prove him wrong? So too, if after long discussion another person continues to condone mercy killing while I condemn it, what is to be done? "After every circumstance, every relation is known," David Hume observed in such cases, "the understanding has no further room to operate, nor any object on which it could employ itself."[6] Divergent *preferences* can hardly be *refuted*.

Here too, however, the tables may be turned on the objector. In any discussion, on any topic, there might come a point where reasons gave out and further debate became futile. Nothing can be proved to a person who will accept nothing that has not been proved. "Not even in pure mathematics, that paradigm of strict security of reasoning," notes Bambrough,

> can we *force* a man to accept our premises or our modes of inference; and therefore we cannot force him to accept our conclusions. Once again the moral scep-

tic counts as a reason for doubting the objectivity of morals a feature of moral enquiry which is exactly paralleled in other departments of enquiry where he does *not* count it as a reason for scepticism. If he is to be consistent, he must either withdraw his argument against the objectivity of morals or subscribe also to an analogous argument against the objectivity of mathematics, physics, history, and every other branch of enquiry.[7]

In confirmation of this counterargument consider again the case of the Melanesians. Doubtless we would find it difficult to persuade them that sharing is better than hoarding and cooperation is preferable to mistrust. But notice the reason. "You would stand a better chance of survival," we perhaps suggest, "if you did more sharing in times of need." "Better!? We would all die of poisoning. You seem to know nothing of our society or of the power of our enemies." "But black magic is not scientific," we object. "'Scientific'?" they reply, in puzzlement or scorn. "What does that mean?" Thus the moral divergence reveals factual disagreement, and the *latter* brings us quickly to the point Hume described, where "the understanding has no further room to operate, nor any object on which it could employ itself." Shall we prove *scientifically* that science is right, to people who do not believe in science? Indeed, one is tempted to turn the tables on Hume and the popular case for moral skepticism, and argue that the only way to disabuse these people of their mistaken *factual* beliefs would be to sell them first on the *merits* of science; and if values thus ground factual beliefs, how can they be less solidly established and hence less objective?

In any case, the second reason, too, is shown to be invalid. The alleged sharp divergence between factual and ethical issues is illusory. Both kinds may lead to intractable disputes. Neither can be resolved in a way that forces assent. Someone can always say, "I disagree with you."

Summing Up

The reasons and responses just considered recall a humorous exchange. Says a doctor to an old-timer: "That pain in your leg is just a matter of old age." Replies the old-timer: "That can't be right, Doc. My other leg is the same age and it doesn't hurt." We laugh. But there is something to the old-timer's reply. It can't be *just* the leg's age that accounts for the ache, for the other leg *is* the same age. Were the explanation adequate, the other should ache too. But it doesn't.

Now that's the way it is if someone says that right and wrong, being subject to disagreement and interminable debates, are therefore mere matters of personal taste. On other questions, too, there is much disagreement. On other questions, too, persuasion proves difficult. Yet *they* are not mere matters of taste, and nobody says they are. So the account cannot be right as it stands. If right and wrong are matters of taste and other questions are not, it must be for some other reason than the two Russell cites. But for what reason? What grounds are there for making that allegation, besides these popular ones?

EXERCISE 1

"On other questions, too [besides moral ones], there is much disagreement. On other questions, too, persuasion proves difficult. Yet *they* are not mere matters of taste, and nobody says they are." For example? List some questions like that concerning the earth's shape, on which there is or has been much disagreement yet which have a right answer, whether or not we know it.

SOURCES OF THE IMPRESSION

If the popular grounds for moral skepticism, when stated and examined, prove so weak, how, you may wonder, did the viewpoint gain such currency? Various explanations suggest themselves, each worth dwelling on. From among them I shall single out three for special attention. Each will reveal a kernel of truth in the skeptical position; yet none will show that moral reasoning is mistaken or unimportant. In this, I believe, they are typical of all the explanations that might be suggested for skepticism's vogue.

A First Source of the Impression: Difficulty

Moral issues are so complex, and people are so ill-prepared to deal with them, that they easily despair of finding a solution, or at least a sure one. And their "Who can say who is right?" therefore expresses as much their doubt about their own and others' abilities as it does concerning the existence of an answer. Indeed, for a great many people the two questions are not distinct. In ethics and often elsewhere they recognize no difference between our being unable to discover a solution and there being none.

In simpler cases the distinction stands out more clearly. Suppose, for example, that we had looked long and hard for the proverbial needle in a haystack and failed to find it. We would not equate our failure with the nonexistence of the object. For we would realize that the haystack is large and the needle very small and our vision quite limited. An eagle or hawk might succeed where we failed.

Somewhat similarly, but closer to our case, those who have searched in vain for a way to harness nuclear fusion have not concluded that no solution exists. The complexity of the problem may bring them close to despair, but they do not infer from their failure that the enterprise is mistaken. Nor do the rest of us. For, ignorant though we are of the details of the problem, we have some sense of its overall complexity. We sense the challenge, without yielding to skepticism concerning a solution or its eventual discovery.

We might adopt a similar attitude toward ethical problems, and be less inclined to moral skepticism, if we realized how closely ethical problems resemble complex problems in physics, sociology, psychology, or elsewhere. For we would then come to see that the ethical problems not only resemble the others but largely coincide with them. And seeing that, we would recognize that no other problems, in any single science, are as difficult as the issues we must often face in ethics. Ethical haystacks are the biggest of all, so the hardest to spot a needle in, so the likeliest to create the impression that there is no needle — unless we realize how immense the problems are.

Consider, for example, the question debated in this country for a decade: "Should we have troops in South Vietnam?" The verdict hinged on a series of subordinate issues, each a major puzzle in itself. For example:

(1) Our involvement was clearly mistaken if there was no hope of a military solution. But was it really possible to win the war? Some said yes; some said no.

(2) Again, most people objected to the tactics sometimes employed — the torture, the massacres, the defoliation, the napalmed villages. But were they a psychological or military necessity? Are atrocities inseparable from warfare? Was victory possible by less savage means? Again, opinions were divided — regarding the facts and regarding the possibilities.

(3) For some we were saving the South Vietnamese from northern, communist oppressors; for others we were imposing our will on a reluctant population. How did the Vietnamese feel? What were their genuine sentiments and preferences? On this vital question, too, opinions diverged.

(4) A further decisive issue was the so-called "Domino Theory." If South Vietnam fell to the communists, would neighboring countries follow? Some argued "Yes"; others argued "No," often simplistically. As the subsequent fate of Laos and Cambodia on the one hand and of Thailand on the other attests, the question was complex. For what were China's true intentions? How relevant was the split between Russia and China? How strong a counter-

force might nationalism prove to be? These related questions were all debatable.

(5) Money, too, was a major consideration. Wouldn't the billions spent on the war achieve far more for the world and more effectively check the spread of communism if spent on foreign aid? Yet what likelihood was there, the other side could counter, that the end of the war would bring any notable increase in foreign aid?

(6) Further debate concerned the relative merits of a democratic versus a nondemocratic (e.g., communist) regime in achieving economic development. Would any people ever freely adopt the curbs on consumption required for capital investment to launch a backward country like Vietnam into economic orbit?

(7) How bad a thing, politically, was communism likely to prove, in Vietnam and roundabout? Were purges and persecutions to be expected, or milder repression, or could communist promises of tolerance be trusted?

(8) How good or bad a thing, in general, was communism? Was it a mere bogeyman, used to frighten us, or was it all our leaders said it was?

This final query may look less factual than the preceding. But break it down, too, and it reveals a similar bundle of factual subissues, each difficult in itself and each decisive for the answer. Is the Marxist reading of history correct? or Marxist economics? or the Marxist view of society as a whole? or the Marxist critique of religion? or the Marxist view of the future? or the verdict that Marxist goals require communist tactics—that is, violent revolution and a subsequent "dictatorship of the proletariat"? Each such issue, as I say, is complex, debatable, and relevant to the overall evaluation of communism as an ideology and historical movement.

Every item in the original list could be broken down this way, and other considerations could be added (what of the Geneva agreements, of our promises to the South Vietnamese, of the chaos created in this country, of the effects on our foreign relations, . . . ?). Problems within problems within problems could be cited, realistically: some for historians to resolve, some for military theorists, some for economists, some for sociologists, some for psychologists, some for political scientists, some for philosophers or theologians, some for specialists from several fields working together. But I imagine the reader can already grasp the truth of the two statements I set out to illustrate.

First, I suggested that complex moral issues not only resemble those in other areas but largely coincide with them. Thus, prove to advocates of intervention that the war could not be won, or communism was a good thing, or was good for Vietnam, or could be checked more effectively by pacific means, and their support would cease. Prove the contrary to opponents of intervention, and their opposition would likely end. Disagreement typically hinged on subissues like those I have listed, themselves strictly factual or largely resolvable into factual questions.

Second, I suggested that complex moral issues, like this one, are more complex than any problem an individual science must resolve. For one thing they require input from many different sciences. For another thing the questions they pose these sciences are often too difficult to answer with any assurance. (It was unclear, for instance, even to experts, whether we could succeed militarily in Vietnam, whether a free or unfree system would favor economic

"The United States is . . . conscious of its responsibility and duty, in its own self-interest as well as the interest of other free peoples, to assist a brave country in the defense of its liberties against unprovoked subversion and Communist terror." — *Lyndon B. Johnson*	"U.S. President Lyndon Johnson [has] spread the smokescreen of independence, freedom, peace, and negotiations in an attempt to whitewash the towering crimes and aggressive and war-seeking policy of the U.S. imperialists in Vietnam." — *Hoan Quoc Viet*

development, whether the South Vietnamese as a whole welcomed or regretted our involvement.) Finally, the varied strands must be woven into a single, overall solution, in accordance with sound theory and the canons of right reasoning.

It is little wonder, therefore, if ordinary mortals, when faced with such complexity, should throw up their hands, half in skepticism, half in despair, and exclaim, "Who is to say which answer is correct?" And this they may easily equate with "Who is to say there is a correct answer?" If nobody can find the needle, who is to say there is one?

A Second Source: Tied Verdicts

Jean-Paul Sartre cites a different sort of example to support the same skeptical conclusion. Though it fails as support, it does reveal another important source of the skeptical attitude so many people harbor, even while, in practice, they debate an issue like Vietnam and declare what should and should not be done.

The case Sartre cites concerns a student who came to him for advice, during the Second World War, under the following circumstances:

> his father was on bad terms with his mother, and, moreover, was inclined to be a collaborationist; his older brother had been killed in the German offensive of 1940, and the young man, with somewhat immature but generous feelings, wanted to avenge him. His mother lived alone with him, very much upset by the half-treason of her husband and the death of her older son; the boy was her only consolation.
>
> The boy was faced with the choice of leaving for England and joining the Free French Forces — that is, leaving his mother behind — or remaining with his mother and helping her to carry on. He was fully aware that the woman lived only for him and that his going-off — and perhaps his death — would plunge

her into despair. He was also aware that every act that he did for his mother's sake was a sure thing, in the sense that it was helping her to carry on, whereas every effort he made toward going off and fighting was an uncertain move which might run aground and prove completely useless; for example, on his way to England he might, while passing through Spain, be detained indefinitely in a Spanish camp; he might reach England or Algiers and be stuck in an office at a desk job. As a result, he was faced with two very different kinds of action: one, concrete, immediate, but concerning only one individual; the other concerned an incomparably vaster group, a national collectivity, but for that very reason was dubious, and might be interrupted en route.[8]

"Who could help him choose?" Sartre asks.

> Christian doctrine? No. Christian doctrine says, "Be charitable, love your neighbor, take the more rugged path, etc., etc." But which is the more rugged path? Whom should he love as a brother? The fighting man or his mother? Which does the greater good, the vague act of fighting in a group, or the concrete one of helping a particular human being to go on living? Who can decide *a priori*? Nobody. No book of ethics can tell him. The Kantian ethics says, "Never treat any person as a means, but as an end." Very well, if I stay with my mother, I'll treat her as an end and not as a means; but by virtue of this very fact, I'm running the risk of treating the people around me who are fighting, as means; and, conversely, if I go to join those who are fighting, I'll be treating them as an end, and, by doing that, I run the risk of treating my mother as a means.

No principles, then, can help us. The young man was on his own. "I had only one answer to give," writes Sartre of his carefully picked sample: "'You're free, choose, that is, invent.'"

The weakness of this example as evidence for skepticism can be shown through a comparison. Suppose I measure two six-foot athletes. The tape measure gives the same result both times, so I can't say which person is taller. But that doesn't mean the measure is unreliable. I need not throw it away and invent an answer on my own, as Sartre suggests. The tape gives no answer to the question "Which is taller?" precisely because it is accurate. Neither *is* taller. The only correct answer is "A tie."

Now the verdict may be the same in Sartre's sample, for the same reason. The moral measures Sartre tries are the Christian norm of charity and the Kantian rule of never treating people as mere means. Applied to one alternative, then the other, neither norm yields a decisive answer, one way or the other. For in the particular case chosen for analysis there may indeed be no answer, any more than there is to the question: "Which of these two six-footers is taller?" The answer, once again, may be "Neither." Neither alternative may be preferable to the other. Both may be equally good or equally bad. When carefully assessed, they may come out even.

This can be seen from Sartre's own analysis. Why, on the one hand, does he stress that "every act that he did for his mother's sake was a sure thing," whereas "every effort he made toward going off and fighting was an uncertain move which might run aground and prove completely useless"? Why, on the other hand, does he point out that one course of action concerned "only one individual," whereas the other concerned "an incomparably vaster group, a national collectivity"? Because that way the answer comes out roughly even. For anyone rates a sure benefit over an unsure one, and anybody rates a benefit to millions over one to a single individual; and the verdict may therefore be a draw when a *sure* benefit to a *single* person weighs on one side of the scales and an *unsure* (participation in

a) benefit to *millions* weighs on the other side. Apply these common measures of right and wrong to a well-chosen sample, and the answer may resemble that for six-footers: "Neither of these equally good actions is clearly better than the other."

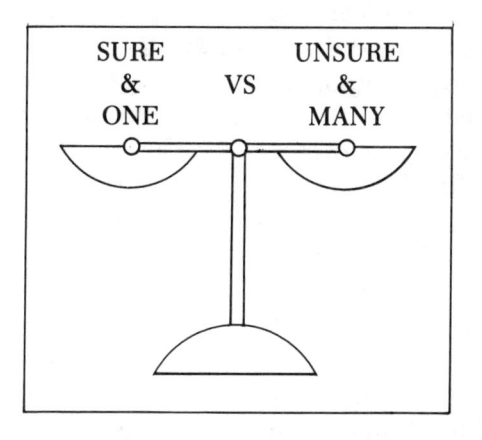

```
┌─────────────────────────────────┐
│   SURE              UNSURE      │
│    &       VS         &         │
│   ONE                MANY       │
│    ◡─────────┬─────────◡        │
│              │                  │
│              │                  │
│             ◠◠◠                 │
└─────────────────────────────────┘
```

Sartre's example, then, though not very telling as a proof for skepticism, reveals another likely source of the skeptical impression. It suggests another reason why the notion might arise that ethical questions, generally, have no answer. In a sense they sometimes don't. The answer — the accurate, objective answer — may sometimes be: "A tie."

A Third Source: Emotional Involvement

Realistic reflection on either of the preceding examples — Vietnam or the student's dilemma — leads to a third likely source of the common impression that ethical questions are mere matters of taste or personal preference. Though questionable in theory, the impression may be accurate enough as a reflection of actual practice. For passion and personal preference often work more powerfully than reason in shaping moral verdicts.

This should come as no surprise. Moral matters are, after all, vital matters. Of their very nature they impinge on our lives, as historical, scientific, or speculative questions frequently do not. The student who consulted Sartre, for example, faced a decision that would crucially affect himself and others. It was his brother the Germans had killed, his father who was collaborating, his mother who would be consoled or desolated. Naturally, then, his emotions were engaged. In a less reflective person they might have swept all reasoning aside. In his case they may have determined the ultimate verdict. Pity for his mother or desire to avenge his brother may have cast the decisive vote when he finally determined "the better thing to do."

In the case of the Vietnam War we need make fewer surmises; we know from experience how people reached their opposing verdicts. For some it was enough to see a picture of a napalmed child: their horror said "Wrong," without benefit of reasoning or complex calculations. For others it was enough to read of communist purges, prisons, brainwashing, people's courts: dread and indignation then answered "Right." Even where discussion occurred, cool objectivity was relatively rare. To cite communist China's conquest of hunger, say, was to invite the label "communist sympathizer"; to mention darker sides of communist practice as possible justification was to risk being classed a hardhearted hawk. Passions ran high, reason ran low, throughout the conflict.

What I am illustrating, perhaps with overemphasis, is a familiar, predictable fact of life. Ethical issues are emotional issues. Whereas, for example, a debate about the causes of cancer generates interest but little passion, a debate about abortion or some current war generates passion as well as interest. Noting the passion and the part it plays in moral judgments, we may legitimately suspect their objectivity. To a greater or lesser extent, "wrong" may look equivalent to "I don't like it," while "right" may seem a variant for "I prefer it." And the impression may be right. As a comment on actual practice, the claim that "ethical judgments are a matter of personal preference" contains much truth.

EXERCISE 2

Identify moral issues, past or present, that compare with this chapter's chief illustrations:

(a) giving the anesthetic or not (simple, clear, uncontested)

(b) joining the Free French or staying home (an apparent draw)

(c) fighting in Vietnam or withdrawing (maximum complexity)

In each instance spell out the resemblance fully, concretely.

PRACTICAL IMPLICATIONS

Together the three factors just discussed — moral complexity, tied verdicts, emotional involvement — go a long way toward explaining the wide currency of moral skepticism. Not only do they explain it, but they partially justify it: they suggest senses in which it contains some truth. Between them, accordingly, they may cast doubt on the legitimacy and worth of moral reasoning. Yet in no instance is this practical inference warranted. In no instance does it follow that we should do less moral reasoning or take it less seriously. For consider the three factors once again, one by one:

(1) The example of Vietnam, with which I started, might appear to confirm Samuel Johnson's verdict:

> Life is not long, and too much of it must not pass in idle deliberation how it shall be spent; deliberation, which those who begin it by prudence, and continue it with subtility, must, after long expence of thought, conclude by chance. To prefer one future mode of life to another, upon just reasons, requires faculties which it has not pleased our Creator to give us.[9]

Moral questions, I suggested, may be more complex than any in a science like astronomy or physics. The search for a verdict on Vietnam may be more difficult than the search for a technique to control nuclear fusion. If, then, the most competent physicists have so far failed in the latter inquiry, what are the chances that mere mortals like ourselves, or even skilled ethicians, can reach clarity on an issue as complex as Vietnam?

In answer I would point out, first of all, that not all moral questions are as difficult as that one. Some are so unproblematic that we don't give them a thought. We don't hesitate a moment, for example (to cite Bambrough's case), whether we should give a child an anesthetic before removing her appendix. Of course we should. Pain is a bad thing, needless agony an evil. Those who think otherwise and delight in inflicting pain we confine with those who believe they are bumblebees. Other cases, to be sure, are more problematic than that of the child. But they need not be as complicated as the Vietnam issue, or as difficult to resolve. Many intermediate degrees of complexity stretch between the simplest and the most difficult cases.

Furthermore, even the most complex questions may be clarified by deliberation. The chances of choosing well are improved by thinking things out. We may not achieve any sudden illumination, like a physicist spotting a trick to harness fusion. But then again we may. It does happen. And the likelihood increases, in ethics as in physics, if we put our minds to the task. Where at first we perceive only impenetrable complexity, we may on closer inspection spot some decisive consideration, for or against the action or policy in question.

(2) From our second example, too, concerning the student's choice, some might conclude with Sartre that no answers are possible. But such despair of moral reasoning is premature. For his sample moral problem, though typical of many, does not represent the majority. Sometimes reflection indicates a tie; oftener it does not. And even when it does, or seems to, then too we have an answer: we have reason to believe that one course of action is as good as the

other. And further reflection might resolve the deadlock. The student might spot some surer way to escape and join the Free French forces, or some way to console his mother without staying by her side.

(3) Actual practice, I suggested, is seldom so fully reflective. Reason, if we used it, might take us far; but with bias and emotion so strong, what are the chances of our reaching objective answers? In matters of life and death — Vietnam, abortion, and the like — who can be dispassionate? Who *should* be?

In answer we may distinguish, first, between passionate interest in an issue and passionate commitment to a verdict; second, between commitment after deliberation and commitment before; third, between cases where deliberation should precede commitment and those where it need not. Consider, for example, the question of giving the girl an anesthetic before her appendectomy. The issue is simple, the verdict uncontested. Without need of deliberation we are committed to an answer and would react with indignation to any contrary suggestion (that is, that we cut her open without an anesthetic). Consider, by contrast, the case of Vietnam. There the issue is more complex, opinions are divided, and error is easy; so commitment without reflection seems mistaken.

Fine in theory, these distinctions will make no difference if they are not applied or acted on. But who is to say they will be? Who is to say that reasoning will in fact precede difficult decisions and not follow them? Who is to say, therefore, that the reasoning will be genuine and not mere rationalization? Who is to say the verdicts will be objective answers, honestly arrived at, and not mere personal preferences or peeves?

Well, we are, to start with. The choice is ours. Will *we* be objective in our thinking, or won't we? Can we be, or can't we? We'll never know unless we try. The proof of the pudding, as they say, is in the eating; the proof of our capacities is in their exercise. A course like the present is as much an invitation, or experiment, as it is a demonstration.

EXERCISE 3

1. These explanations work well enough for the chapter's favorite paradigms—Vietnam, the student, the child's appendectomy—and moral reasoning therefore seems vindicated. But will the same explanations work equally well in other cases, for instance those cited for exercise 2? Consider the issues you listed under a, b, and c, and ask: Might they give rise to similar misgivings, and might the misgivings be similarly answered?

2. To review the whole chapter, answer the following questions:

   a. What is "moral skepticism"?

   b. What two grounds seem to support it?

   c. What is the flaw in both these arguments?

   d. How might the difficulty of moral questions create a skeptical impression?

   e. How might cases like the one Sartre cites?

   f. How might people's emotional involvement in moral issues?

   g. What kernels of truth do these three sources reveal in the skeptical impression?

   h. Why, nonetheless, does none of the three—not the first, nor the second, nor the third—invalidate moral reasoning?

CHAPTER 3
Sound Moral Arguments

Regrettable though it may seem, such is life. If you want to be a physicist, you have to master calculus. If you want to be a pianist or a singer, you have to do your scales. If you want to be a successful boxer, you have to spar and jog. And if you want to reach sound moral verdicts—on nuclear arms, abortion, reverse discrimination, or any other subject of vital interest—you have to learn the ABCs of sound moral reasoning.

In part that means learning some logic. What, in general, makes reasoning strong, what makes it weak? Which patterns of inference assure success, which do not? Which forms look reliable but cannot be trusted? What fallacies lie in wait for the unwary thinker? Such are the questions a course in logic pursues, to facilitate sound reasoning in any field of inquiry.

A book of ethics, like this, cannot treat these questions as thoroughly as a book of logic would; this chapter and the next will just make a few basic points, simply and concisely. By way of compensation, though, the treatment can focus more sharply on strictly moral reasoning than a logic text usually does, and more specifically still on *moral arguments*. An explanation of the expression "moral argument" will make clear the reason for this sharper focus adopted throughout this chapter and the next.

MORAL ARGUMENTS

By "argument" logicians and ethicians do not usually mean a quarrel or debate, but a case made out on one side or the other of some issue. In the abortion controversy, for example, various such arguments are urged on both sides, some for and some against the practice. One of the simplest goes as follows:

> (1) It is always wrong to take innocent human life.
> Fetal life is innocent human life.
> Therefore it is wrong to take fetal life.

A typical counterargument would be:

> (2) The fetus is part of a woman's body.
> A woman may dispose of her body as she pleases.
> Therefore she may abort the fetus if she desires.

In each of these samples the first two propositions are cited as evidence, or grounds, for the third. The supported proposition is called the *conclusion,* the supporting propositions are called the *premises,* and the whole *argument* consists of the premises together with the conclusion.

An argument's conclusion need not come at the end. It might, for instance, occur at the beginning: "*It is wrong to take fetal life,* since it is always wrong to take innocent human life, and fetal life is innocent human life." Or the conclusion might appear in the middle of the argument: "It is always wrong to take innocent human life; so *it is wrong to take fetal life,* since fetal life is innocent human life." From these same examples it is clear that premises too have no one position. What makes a proposition a premise is not its coming first or last or in the middle, but its being asserted as evidence for a conclusion.

Notice: its being *asserted* as evidence. For other people may not agree that it does, and it may in fact do little or nothing to support the conclusion. Still, what holds for reasoning holds for arguments: as bad reasoning is still reasoning, so a bad argument is still an argument. The propositions *offered* as evidence are the argument's premises; the proposition *alleged* to follow from them is the argument's conclusion, whether or not it does in fact draw support from them.

What makes an argument a *moral argument*, good or bad, is its having a moral proposition as its conclusion. The issue debated is a moral one, and the verdict argued to is a moral verdict. In the manner described in chapter 1, the conclusion asserts what is right or wrong, permissible or impermissible. Thus the sample arguments above are moral arguments, not because their premises are moral propositions (as the first in fact is, in both instances), but because their conclusions make moral claims: "It is *wrong* to take fetal life," "A woman *may* abort the fetus if she desires." In each case the argument addresses and decides a moral issue.

Notice, therefore, that a moral argument is not moral in the same sense that an action, person, or institution is moral. To call such things moral is to praise or approve of them; to call an argument moral is simply to classify it. The label marks off one type of reasoning from others. As scientific arguments concern scientific matters and political arguments concern political matters, so arguments that address moral issues are moral arguments. Whether they argue well or badly, such is their classification the moment they draw a verdict concerning some moral question.

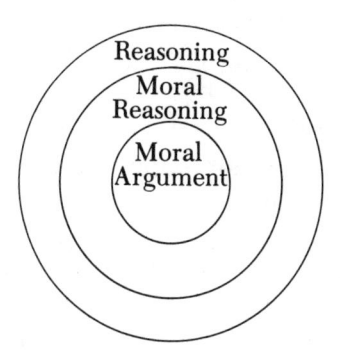

```
        Reasoning
        Moral
       Reasoning
        Moral
       Argument
```

PATTERNS OF ARGUMENT

Moral reasoning, we saw in chapter 1, looks for an answer, and may or may not find one. Moral arguments do. They reach a verdict. They say what is right or wrong. Hence their interest for a study of ethics. If they are strong, so is the position they support. If they are weak (and no stronger ones can be found), so is the position they favor. It follows, therefore, that in order to assess moral verdicts, we must be able to assess the strength of the arguments that support them.

How, then, is the strength or weakness of a moral argument to be gauged? The first step, as in assessing any argument, is to recognize its pattern or structure. Most basically, we must accurately identify its conclusion and the premises used to support it. If we mistake the conclusion for a premise and a premise for the conclusion, the argument, no matter how strong, will look exceedingly weak. Our sample arguments (1) and (2), for example, though not very strong, would look still weaker than they are if we turned them around and supposed they were arguing from a single instance to all instances — that is, from the specific wrongness just of abortion to the universal wrongness of taking innocent life, or from the specific right to abort to the universal right to dispose of one's body as one wishes. The inference from one case to all is a risky leap; the inference from all to one is not.

Of course we wouldn't read either argument that weaker way, and don't; for they wouldn't make sense if so construed. Besides, clear connectives indicate each time where to look for the conclusion, where for the premises. In the initial, indented versions of the arguments, "therefore" points ahead to the conclusion; in the second and third versions of argument (1) "since" and "for" point ahead to premises, with the clear implication that the conclusion has just been stated. Other arguments, however, contain no such explicit clues; indeed the conclusion may not be explicitly stated. In such instances we must discern the general drift of the reasoning so as to identify what is argued from and what is argued to.

Once we have detected the pattern of an argument, we can picture the pattern. Suppose, for instance, there were just a single premise:

    (3) The fetus has a soul.
        Therefore it should not be killed.

Using the letter "p" for the premise and the letter "c" for the conclusion, we might depict their relation like this:

$$\begin{array}{c} \text{\textcircled{p}} \\ | \\ \text{\textcircled{c}} \end{array}$$

The downward line represents dependence. Hence, where two premises support the conclusion, as in arguments (1) and (2), two lines might be used:

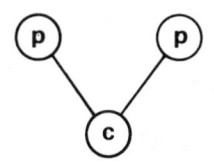

$$\begin{array}{c} \text{\textcircled{p}} \quad \text{\textcircled{p}} \\ \diagdown \diagup \\ \text{\textcircled{c}} \end{array}$$

For three supporting premises there would be three lines, for four four, and so forth.

Sometimes, however, a premise supports the conclusion only indirectly, its immediate job being to bolster some premise. Such a subpremise appears, for example, in the following argument:

    (4) The fetus has done nothing to merit its extinction.
        Therefore it is innocent.
        Therefore it should not be aborted.

Here the first premise supports the second, and the second supports the conclusion. So the appropriate scheme would be:

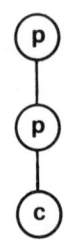

```
(p)
 |
(p)
 |
(c)
```

The diagram would be still clearer if it showed which premise depends on which, and which directly supports the conclusion. So we might number the premises in the order of their appearance and diagram the argument as follows:

```
(1)
 |
(2)
 |
(c)
```

Other, more complex patterns can be diagramed by combining simpler figures like those above. Consider, for instance, the argument:

> (5) The fetus has done nothing to merit its extinction.
> So it is innocent.
> Furthermore it has a soul.
> Therefore it should not be aborted.

Here the first premise supports the second, as in the preceding argument, but the second premise is then joined by the third, and both support the final conclusion. The overall configuration therefore looks as follows (numbering the premises once again, in the order of their appearance, to make clear which premise is which):

```
    1
    |
    2       3
     \     /
       c
```

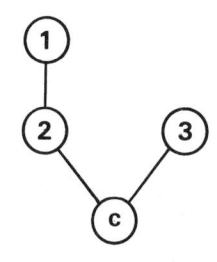

The more complicated an argument's structure, the more evident are the advantages of such diagraming. A diagram pictures clearly what might otherwise remain a confused jumble of propositions. And the task it sets assures that the jumble gets untangled. So long as a single operative proposition — premise, subpremise, or conclusion — is not accounted for, the diagram is not complete. The demands of accurate representation permit no fudging, no easygoing assumption that we know how the argument functions when in fact we have not deciphered the relation of part to part.

Still, the diagram is just a means, not an end in itself. It is just a handy way to achieve a clearer view. If it does that, fine; if not, forget it and attend to the argument. There is no use debating whether the diagram should be drawn one way or another if the argument's structure is already sufficiently clear. Frequently, though, doubt about the picture reflects doubt about the argument. And until that uncertainty is resolved, the argument cannot be evaluated. We cannot judge whether an argument succeeds or fails until we know what it *is*. And that we do not know simply by knowing its parts.

EXERCISE 1

Identify the conclusion, then the premise(s) of each argument; then number the premise(s) and diagram the argument's structure. Notice that a single sentence may state a premise and a conclusion, or state several premises, making distinct points.

a. I shouldn't criticize them. For I have done the same things myself.

b. Since others have a right to their reputation, we should not reveal their secret faults.

c. I don't need the money, and my patients are poor; so I shouldn't charge such high fees.

d. Since smoking harms the smoker, and the smoke annoys others, smoking is wrong.

e. You owe your parents a great deal; for they gave you life, they raised you, they educated you. Therefore you should care for them in their old age.

f. Graft is immoral; for it breeds dishonesty, and dishonesty is a canker of society.

g. Without voting there is no democracy. Hence we should vote. For democracy is preferable to other forms of government.

h. Animals have feelings, as you and I do. Indeed their senses are keener than ours. But experimental procedures are often painful. Animals, therefore, should not be used for experimental purposes.

i. No war is now licit. For once war starts, nuclear weapons will be used. And the use of nuclear weapons cannot be justified. They are far too destructive.

j. People are sometimes selfish, and sometimes they are misguided. So their desires do not always coincide with the common good. But the common good should be the chief concern of legislators. It follows therefore that legislators should not always accede to the desires of their constituents.

REAL-LIFE ARGUMENTS

All the sample arguments served up so far have, as it were, been filleted in advance. Head, fins, and tail have been lopped off, and the bones have been extracted. Only pure meat remains, ready to cut and eat. Real-life arguers, however, are seldom so considerate. To prepare their arguments for analysis and evaluation, we must generally do some cleaning and paring. Introductory remarks, repetitions, peripheral observations, and surplus verbiage must be cut away, and questions or exhortations must be reworded as propositions, when such is their sense. Only then will the verbal fish be ready for the fork.

Consider, for instance, the passage from which the preceding exercise's first argument was extracted. When Sparky Anderson was manager of the Cincinnati Reds, he was quoted as saying:

> After a pennant-clinching, the players are supposed to salute each other's performance, enjoy their victory and maybe take a couple of sips of champagne. But do they? Of course not. They throw it all around the clubhouse, douse everybody with it and what not. You see how they carry on, the wild way they act.
>
> If the players do this, why not the fans? I did the same things. I'm no better than them. Here I am calling them animals and lunatics and I'm doing the same thing. How can I sit here and criticize the behavior of the fans when mine isn't any better?[1]

At first glance you might not notice any argument here. But the closing question is rhetorical, and its sense clearly is: I shouldn't criticize them. And the reason, as clearly, is: I have acted the same way myself. There is the whole argument. The remarks about the players, for example, do not function as premises in this particular bit of reasoning. For Sparky had not criticized the players, but the fans. He had complained of their wild behavior. And now he was blaming himself for letting off steam. He had no right to blame the crowd, he said, since he himself had behaved the same way.

Sometimes, then, the conclusion of an argument may be veiled as a question. Other times it takes the form of an invitation, exhortation, or command ("Let's do this!" "Don't do that!"). Often it is not stated but is left implicit. Or it is tucked into a subordinate clause or phrase from which it had better be extracted for clear recognition. For example: "The boy replies that of course *he should steal*, *as life is more important than money.*" Here the conclusion is the italicized bit. The main clause, "The boy replies," forms no part of the argument; it just introduces it.

Thus relatively few moral arguments you will meet later in this text or elsewhere formulate their verdicts as neatly and explicitly as do those in exercise 1. People convey their moral convictions in endlessly varied ways. The following letter to *Time* offers a typical sampling:

> I was shocked to read that some doctors advise their patients with herpes not to warn prospective sexual partners about their condition. Shame on them. This advice will contribute to the spread of an incurable disease, and it will inflict upon herpes sufferers additional guilt and psychological trauma if they transmit herpes to innocent victims through deceit and lies. Such advice is reckless and unprofessional.

"I was shocked," "shame on them," "reckless and unprofessional"—these varied expressions, though perhaps not strictly ethical, leave no doubt as to where the writer stands. Doctors, he contends, should not give such advice. So a simplified version of the argument might read:

> (6) Advising patients with herpes not to warn prospective sexual partners about their condition will contribute to the spread of this incurable disease.
> And it will inflict upon herpes sufferers additional guilt and psychological trauma if they transmit herpes to innocent victims through deceit and lies.
> Therefore doctors should not so advise their patients.

The presence of varied expressions of disapproval in an argument may lay a trap for unwary analyzers. If you fail to notice that the moral conclusion appears more than once, in varying guises, you are likely to list one or the other of its formulations as an extra premise supporting the conclusion. In the argument just quoted, for example, you might cite the final sentence ("Such advice is reckless and unprofessional") as a further reason for condemning the doctor's advice, whereas it is in fact just a variant version of the condemnation, adding nothing to the grounds already cited.

The following argument, from Jean Jacques Rousseau's *The New Eloise*, proves equally tricky for different reasons and has further lessons to teach concerning the analysis of real-life arguments:

> To seek happiness and avoid misery in that which does not affect another is a natural right. When our life is misery for us and is not a pleasure for anyone, it is therefore permissible to free ourselves from it.

The word "therefore," placed as it is halfway through the final sentence, sets a trap for the unwary. It might just as well have opened the whole sentence, thus clearly connecting the premise in the first sentence with the conclusion in the second. As it is, however, many students, even when forewarned, suppose that what follows "therefore" is the conclusion of the argument and what precedes it, in the first clause, is a premise. And this assumption is seriously mistaken, for several important reasons, each worth dwelling on.

First, the opening clause—"When our life is misery for us and is not a pleasure for anyone"—cannot be a premise in the argument, since it makes no assertion. It does not say our life is miserable, has been miserable, or ever will be miserable (though it may imply it). It just indicates *when* it would be permissible to end our lives. It modifies the final clause. So anyone inclined to reckon such a nonassertion as a premise should recall that premises are "supporting *propositions*" (to quote from earlier). One way or another they make a claim, say something true or false. This "when" clause does not.

To make sure, then, that a premise really is a premise you had better word it as a full, independent assertion. In one text you may spot a subordinate clause as a possible premise (think of some clauses in exercise 1 starting with "since"), in another a noun phrase (e.g., "the cost and horrors of war"), in another a rhetorical question (e.g., "Would you want somebody to treat you that way?"). Whatever the grammatical construction, if you can reword it as a complete declarative sentence without falsifying the author's meaning, you may be right in taking it for a premise. Otherwise not.

The analysis that makes the "when" clause a premise goes wrong in a second way worth noting. Premises are not only propositions, statable in declarative sentences, but *supporting* propositions. And that opening clause, since it makes no assertion, does not and cannot support any conclusion. If no claim is made, no inference can be drawn from it. So if you are inclined to treat some doubtful item as a premise, add a second question to the first. Ask not only whether the construction makes an assertion; ask also whether it lends any support to the conclusion you are inclined to link it with. Does the author think it does? Is that its function in the argument?

Finally, the faulty analysis falsifies the argument in still a third way. Not only does it treat as a premise what is not a premise, but it thereby lops off an essential part of the conclusion. Deprived of the qualifying clause "When life is misery for us and is not a pleasure for anyone," the conclusion appears to sanction any suicide, without regard for circumstances. It makes no difference, it would seem to imply, whether you are miserable or happy, useless or indispensable: you may do away with yourself if you please. But that is not what the argument says, nor does it follow from the premise in the first sentence. Only the complete second sentence does.

If, then, students often cite just the last clause of this passage from Rousseau as the conclusion of the argument, one more word of warning may be required: Be sure that when you pick out a conclusion, or a premise, you have the whole of it. The wording and order of a text are not sacrosanct. Much may be altered, much may be dropped. But be careful not to trim off any idea — any word or phrase or clause — that makes a difference to the argument.

As all kinds of fish — some finny, some bony, some mostly head — swim in the seas, so arguments of every description occur in moral discourse. But these few samples from among many may give you some idea of the filleting process. Here are others, now, to try your hand on.

EXERCISE 2

For each argument below, proceed as follows: (a) identify the conclusion, then the premise or premises, here in the text; (b) write out your own streamlined version of the argument, as in (6) above, using complete sentences, with the conclusion at the end; (c) number the premise(s) in this written version; (d) diagram the resulting argument, using the numbers. Thus your treatment of an argument should resemble this sample handling of that argument in *Time*:

(1) Advising patients with herpes not to warn prospective partners about their condition will contribute to the spread of this incurable disease.
(2) And it will inflict upon herpes sufferers additional guilt and psychological trauma if they transmit herpes to innocent victims through deceit and lies.
(C) Therefore doctors should not so advise their patients.

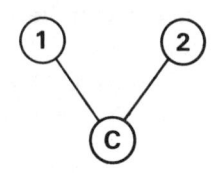

Keep the results for use in exercise 4.

    a. "The use of addictive drugs is immoral because of their disastrous personal and social consequences."
> (Austin Fagothey, *Right and Reason*)

    b. "A justification for fraud that is sometimes offered is: 'If I don't swindle him, my competitor will.'"
> (Sharp and Fox, *Business Ethics*)

    c. "'Give your children a couple of *dis*advantages,' he would say. 'The reason you have things now is because your lack of them as a child spurred you to strive for them.'"
> (Earl Wilson, "Unforgettable Sam Levenson")

    d. "Some competitors use inflated suggestive retail prices so that sellers can convince the buyer that he is getting a real bargain when the price on the tag is dramatically marked down. ... Such procedures harm not only the consumer, but honest competitors, so that they are doubly unethical."
> (Thomas Garrett, *Business Ethics*)

    e. "The old do not have a right to expect their children to care for them even if they have conceived and helped their children through the youth years. I don't know of many parents who had children simply to be assured of providers later in their life."
> (Letter to *U.S. Catholic,* July 1980)

    f. "Suppose ... that I am contemplating evading the payment of income taxes. I might reason that I need the money more than the government does, that the amount I have to pay is so small in comparison with the total amount to be collected that the government will never miss it."
> (Marcus Singer, *Generalization in Ethics*)

    g. "Here's an example to test these skills on. Somebody puts forth the argument that giving people bad grades is a form of punishment, indeed sometimes quite a severe form of punishment as far as their career or scholarship plans are concerned, and that associating education with punishment is a surefire way to turn people off it. Therefore, the arguer concludes, grades should be abolished."
> (Michael Scriven, *Reasoning*)

h. "The Marquis de Sade reasoned that since man was determined and essentially a machine, anything that he might do that he found pleasurable he should do."
(Raymond Gastil, "The Moral Right of the Majority to Restrict Obscenity and Profanity through Law")

i. "Under no circumstances can we inflict violence on people, torture or kill them because we think such acts could be of use to us or to others. We cannot and may not do such things, especially because we can never be sure of the results of our actions. Often actions which seem the most advantageous of all turn out in fact to be destructive; and the reverse is also true."
(Leo Tolstoy, "Advice to a Draftee")

j. "In 1957 a report was produced in England by the Wolfenden Committee. This committee had been established in 1954 in response to complaints that aspects of English law dealing with homosexuality and prostitution were ineffective and unjust. . . . The clear intent of the committee was to say that unless it could be shown that public indecency or personal exploitation were involved, the law should not prohibit activities such as homosexuality and prostitution. Their justification for this recommendation, which is both legal and ethical in character, was simply that the state does not and should not have the right to restrict any private moral actions which affect only the consenting adults involved. The state should not have this right, they argued, because of the supreme importance both social ethics and law place on 'individual freedom of choice and action in matters of private morality . . . which is, in brief and crude terms, not the law's business.'"
(Tom L. Beauchamp, Ethics and Public Policy)

k. "Theologians believe that when a man pounds another into helplessness, scars his face, smashes his nose, jars his brain and exposes it to lasting damage, or when he enters a contest where this could happen to him, he has surpassed the bounds of reasonable stewardship of the human person. Surely there are equally — or more — effective ways for men to learn the art of self-defense."
(Richard McCormick, "Is Professional Boxing Immoral?")

THE STRENGTH OF ARGUMENTS

Analysis like the preceding sets the stage for evaluation. Once we have identified the premises cited for a conclusion and have traced their relation to it, we can assess the argument's force. For the strength or weakness of any argument depends entirely, first on the strength of the premises thus identified, second on the strength of their connection with the conclusion, set forth in the diagram. Are the premises true? If they were, would they prove the conclusion? On the answers to these two questions, and on them alone, depends the soundness of the argument.

Some premises are clearly true, some clearly false, many in between. Some connections are clearly conclusive, others clearly not, many in between. And the two factors — premise strength and connection strength — vary independently. Thus the premises of an argument may be evidently true, but their connection with the conclusion very weak; or the connection may be airtight, but the premises clearly false. To illustrate these two possibilities with extreme if farfetched clarity, consider the following two arguments.

First: "Grapes are fruit, and rain falls from clouds, so Elizabeth Taylor must be the queen of England." Clearly there is something wrong with this argument. Yet the premises are both true. Grapes *are* fruit; no doubt about it. And rain *does* fall from clouds. The problem is, how do these two premises, singly or together, prove that Elizabeth Taylor is the queen of England? What do grapes have to do with British royalty? The *connection* is weak, indeed nonexistent.

Now consider a second bit of reasoning: "All pets are fish, and all fish have fur, so all pets have fur." This argument, you can sense, is as worthless as the first; but the reason is exactly the opposite. This time it is the premises that are weak and the connection that is strong. *If* all pets were fish and all fish had fur, as alleged, it would follow ineluctably that all pets have fur. The connection could not be stronger, but the premises are both clearly *false*. It is not true that all pets are fish. It is not true that all fish have fur.

The distinction between premise strength and connection strength, though simple and basic, proves difficult for some to grasp. So consider this comparison. If a parachute is large enough, it will support a parachutist — provided the cords connecting it to him are strong. Again, if the connecting strands are sturdy, they will hold him up — provided the parachute is large enough. But the largest parachute will do no good if attached by spider webs, and a two-inch hawser will do no good if attached to a hanky-sized parachute. For a successful descent both things are necessary: strong strands, large parachute.

Now that's the way it is with arguments. The strongest, truest premises will not prove a conclusion if not logically related to it; the tightest logical connection will do no good if the premises are false. In the argument on Elizabeth Taylor the premises are sure, but the connection is thinner than thread. In the argument on pets the connection is unbreakable, but the premises are clearly false, so furnish no support.

EXERCISE 3

To develop familiarity with the distinction between premise strength and connection strength, draw up arguments of your own in which:

(a) the premises are strong, the connection weak (as in the argument about Elizabeth Taylor);

(b) the connection is strong, the premises weak (as in the argument on pets);

(c) both the premises and the connection are weak;

(d) both the premises and the connection are strong.

EVALUATING ARGUMENTS

The ideal in argumentation, naturally, is to have both foolproof premises and airtight connections. But that combination is rare. After all, were the case that strong and evident, who would need to make it? Arguments are aired when people feel uncertain or disagree. And in that case some premise or other, or some connection, typically proves problematic.

In argument (1), for example, it might be questioned whether it is always wrong to take innocent human life. What if innocent lives must be lost whichever way one acts? What of ectopic pregnancies, say, where either the fetus must die or both fetus and mother will die? In argument (2) it might be contested whether the fetus is part of a woman's body—at least in any sense that gives her the right to dispose of it as she pleases. (See chapter 4.)

Beginners often do too little questioning and accept quite controversial claims without a quibble. Or, being at a loss what judgment to render on a premise, they may take the easy way out and remark: "Some say this, some say that; opinions differ." However, mere citation of opinions carries no weight; it gives no answer, especially when the views conflict. So in the exercises to come, try to be realistic. Adopt the attitude you naturally would if faced by an important decision or called on to agree or disagree concerning some matter of vital interest to you. If asked "Will you marry me?" or required to register for the draft, or faced with the choice of a college to attend, you would not indulge in the "Some say this, some say that" routine. You would try to determine the better thing to do. Take the same approach here.

With regard to connections the chief thing to guard against is taking premises singly rather than together. This would clearly be an error in the case of an argument like (1) or (2). Neither premise singly, no matter how true, would give the conclusion any support, whereas between them they would assure its truth. If, as alleged, it is always wrong to take innocent human life, *and* fetal life is innocent human life, then it follows more surely than night follows day that it is wrong to take fetal life. The connection is airtight. If, on the contrary, the fetus is part of a woman's body, *and* a woman has a right to dispose of her own body, it follows with like necessity that she has a right to abort the fetus if she wishes. In such instances as these, where each premise pulls no weight without the other, the only way to accurately assess the strength of the connection is to consider both premises together.

The same rule holds for premises that work independently (like multiple parachutes), each giving the conclusion some support, though perhaps not enough one by one but only when working together. Suppose, to illustrate, that I called Rome a wonderful city and backed my assertion by citing its parks and squares and fountains, its shops and restaurants, its churches and basilicas and catacombs and climate and lively crowds, its monuments and antiquities and museums, its history and hills and marvelous views, its nearness to sea and mountain, its surrounding countryside, . . . And suppose someone objected that parks do not make a wonderful city, nor do squares, nor do fountains, nor does any other item in my list. "To be sure," I might reply, "no one item proves my point, but put them all together and they do." If all I've said is true, then Rome is indeed a wonderful city. The connection holds.

The same point appears, for example, in argument (6):

The fetus has done nothing to merit its own extinction.
So it is innocent.
And it has a soul.
Therefore it should not be killed.

If the fetus were innocent but had no soul — well, so are tadpoles innocent. If it had a soul but were an unjust aggressor against its mother, then too the argument would be weak. The question we must ask, to assess fairly the strength of the connection, is whether the conclusion would follow if *both* premises were true.

Whether premises work independently, then, or

whether they work together, in either case we must consider them jointly in order to judge their demonstrative force. We may not run through them one by one and declare each time "Too weak," "Too weak," "Too weak." That way we would find fault with even the strongest connections.

The point being so important, I shall reinforce it syntactically: when discussing the soundness of an argument, I shall speak, in the singular, of the premises' *connection* with the conclusion rather than of their connections with it. The question will always be: How much support do they give it *collectively*?

EXERCISE 4

In some argument of exercise 2, already analyzed, assess the solidity of the premises, then of the connection. Keep the two steps distinct. In the first consider all the premises one by one (including the subpremises, if there are any) and ask if they are true. Then, in the second step consider all the premises collectively and ask how strongly they support the conclusion: If they were true, would it be true? Keep the results of this exercise for later consultation in exercise 5.

A STANDARD PROCEDURE

The preceding explanations trace several basic steps, first of analysis, then of evaluation, to assess the soundness of an argument. Analysis locates the conclusion, then the premises, then the links between them. Evaluation checks the truth of the premise(s) and, separately, the strength of the connection. From this double appraisal an overall verdict can emerge.

A standard procedure that may therefore be adopted in critiquing moral arguments consists of the following four components:

Analysis:
1. A streamlined version of the argument, with premises numbered.
2. A diagram of the argument, using the numbers.

Evaluation:
3. Assessment of the premise(s), number by number.
4. Assessment of the connection.

It will generally be better to do as we have done in this chapter and firm up the analytic part, in class, before attempting evaluation. Otherwise the final, evaluative part may go far astray, and much time and effort may be wasted.

To give a better idea of the final result, a composite view of one sample argument may be helpful. Here, then, is how a four-unit account might look for the brief argument detected at the end of Sparky Anderson's remarks:

1. *Streamlined Version*:
   (1) I have done the same things myself.
   (C) Therefore I shouldn't criticize the fans.

2. *Diagram*:

   ①
   │
   ↓
   Ⓒ

3. *Evaluation of the Premise(s)*:
   Sparky knows how he himself has behaved, and so do numerous bystanders. It may be doubted, though, whether his behavior was ever as riotous as that of the fans he berated. They had done extensive damage.

4. *Evaluation of the Connection*:
   The connection, too, looks weak, between the single premise and the argument's conclusion. A

more relevant consideration, I would say, than Sparky's own conduct is whether criticism would improve the crowd's behavior. If it would just cause hard feelings, it would be ill-advised. If it would do some good, and no comparable harm, it would be legitimate, no matter how badly Sparky himself had behaved. To avoid hypocrisy, he could open his criticism with an admission that he was no better than others.

These are my sample remarks; you, no doubt, might have others to make concerning the premise's truth or its connection with the conclusion.

Most arguments are more complex than Sparky's. Several in part two, for example, have this slightly more elaborate structure:

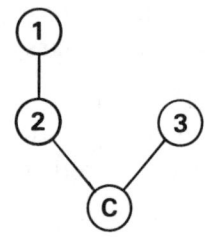

Here there are two premises and one subpremise to assess for truth or falsehood, in step 3. Since 2 is supported by 1, assessment of 2's truth will require considering not only the truth of 1 but also its connection with 2. That will leave just the final connection, between 2 and 3 and the conclusion, to consider in step 4.

This way of handling more complex arguments simplifies the question of connection at the end. Rather than ask, "If the premises *and subpremises* were all true, would the conclusion also be true?" we can ask more pointedly, "If the premises *directly supporting the conclusion* were true, would the conclusion be true?" For that final link is decisive. If it is weak, so is the whole argument. If it is strong, any weakness must come from the premises: one or the other, or several, must be false or uncertain. And that we can learn in step 3, as just described. Between them, therefore, these two critiques — one of truth and the other of connection — cover the ground.

With this point clarified, the overall procedure can now be restated as follows: (1) state the argument fully and concisely; (2) diagram it; (3) assess the truth of the premises and any subpremises; (4) assess the strength of the premises' (not the subpremises') connection with the conclusion. In step 3 take the premises one by one; in step 4 consider them collectively.

Doubtless this four-step procedure is more painstaking than any you have been following, for even the weightiest decisions. So, as Michael Scriven remarks in *Reasoning* (a book recommended as background reading here in part one),

> you won't find your speed in logical analysis going up at first. It will go down. When swimmers or tennis players come under the guidance of a professional coach for the first time, they are often disappointed to find that they have to change the way they were doing things, and they think the new way feels more awkward, doesn't work as well. But the coach has seen a basic flaw in the approach and knows that unless it is corrected, good and quick performance will never be attained by the pupil. In the same way here, although in the end we shall have sharpened up your logical wits and your instinctive reasoning skills so that you can react much more quickly and accurately than now, at first you'll have to go slower than ever before, just to get the steps right.

In the process you will examine important moral issues and learn more about them. For notice that evaluation as comprehensive as that just outlined, though it focuses on a single line of argument, opens broader vistas. Examining Sparky's simple argument, for instance, we are led straight to the heart of the issue itself. Is one's personal behavior what legitimizes criticism? Or is likely benefit a more decisive consideration? Or does it suffice that the criticism be true? The strength of the connection between Sparky's premise and his conclusion cannot be assessed without raising and answering such questions as these. And they in turn may take us far.

FROM THE ARGUMENT INTO THE ISSUE

To assure this broader relevance, a further step may complete the preceding ones, and naturally will, any time we demonstrate the weakness of an argument without thereby resolving the issue it addresses. Sometimes an answer emerges from our critique; sometimes it doesn't, and we are therefore led to ask: Can the argument we have scrutinized be strengthened? Would some other succeed where it has failed? Or do still weightier reasons point to the opposite conclusion? In short, what is the most convincing case that might be made out one way or the other? The analysis and evaluation of the defective argument can serve as a warm-up for this final inquiry.

Not that all will be clear sailing, even then. The arguments proposed and verdicts reached will differ from member to member of a class. Concerning Sparky's criticism, for example, one person might write:

> Sparky was popular, and respected by the fans.
> So his word would carry weight.
> Though some might resent his criticism, others would admire him for it.
> So the results of his criticism would be beneficial overall, and his action was therefore legitimate.

Another might argue, to the contrary:

> The fans who needed straightening out were the rowdiest ones.

> But the rowdiest fans were the ones least likely to listen.
> They would just resent Sparky's words, as preachy interference.
> So it would be better for him to save his breath.

Such a confrontation need not result in an impasse. At least both arguers agree in their basic approach. Both look to the results of the criticism and try to sum them up. But one person thinks the good effects would outweigh the bad, while the other thinks the opposite. So how about it: Would the fans most in need of the criticism be least affected by it? Would the chief result therefore be resentment? Would no foreseeable benefit tip the scales the other way?

Notice that neither person's argument takes the easy way out and says:

> If Sparky thinks his criticism would do more good than harm, he should go ahead.
> If he thinks it would do more harm than good, he should desist.

Nor does either advise, more generally and vaguely still:

> Sparky should do whatever he thinks is right.
> If he thinks it right to criticize the fans, that's what he should do.
> If he thinks it wrong, he shouldn't.

These are answers to a different type of question, about which we have few problems. To be sure, Sparky should do what he thinks is right. On that we all agree. But is his judgment correct? Are his reasons sound? These objective questions are the ones that shall concern us, for they alone are troublesome. When a person asks: "Should I criticize? Should I fight? Should I lie? Should I seek a divorce? Should I grease a palm or two to make the deal go through?" it is no help to reply: "Do whatever you think is right." What *is* right, and *why*? That is what a person typically wishes and needs to know.

78 Sound Moral Arguments

EXERCISE 5

Draw up your own argument, as above, on some issue in exercise 1 or 2 for which the argument there seems defective and on which you believe you can argue more convincingly. Yours may then be one of the arguments, on various issues, chosen for class discussion and evaluation.

A variant: in exercise 1 or 2 let all members of the class individually address the same issue in the same argument, then compare their arguments, identify the points of agreement and disagreement, and try to resolve the disagreements so as to reach a verdict.

CHAPTER 4

Analysis and Charity— Twin Instruments of Truth

The guidelines briefly sketched in chapter 3 may suffice for the arguments in its exercises. Real-life arguments, however, are seldom so simple. The passages tend to be longer, the premises more numerous, the structures more complex. In various ways and for various reasons, the conclusion or premises or both may be difficult to identify, interpret, or state. And evaluation, whether of premises or connections, may pose further puzzles, requiring more guidance than chapter 3 offers.

Later chapters, in part two, will help with evaluation. This one will treat the preliminary analytic task of correctly identifying, interpreting, and wording conclusions and premises. We shall not enter into details. For discussion should not bog down in analysis but move on briskly to evaluation. And this it can generally do with the help of a teacher. Some matters, though, are too important and difficult to be dealt with in passing, so they will receive attention here.

Ambiguities, in particular, often prove both crucial and difficult to deal with. Taken in one sense a conclusion may be acceptable and true, in another not. Read one way the conclusion follows from the premises, read another way it doesn't. Premises themselves, more frequently than conclusions, are open to different interpretations. One reading makes a premise true, another doesn't. One makes it relevant to the conclusion, another makes it irrelevant. And sometimes the sense that makes it true is not the same as makes it relevant, nor the sense that makes it relevant the same as makes it true. So which of the two meanings should we enter in our analysis, then assess for truth and relevance when we come to evaluation?

The present chapter will first offer a guiding principle to handle such cases, then illustrate it fully, and finally provide much practice in its use. The concluding section will, in fact, be something more than practice. It will not be a mere dress rehearsal for more serious inquiries. For the issues addressed in its samples are important, and so are the ambiguities spotted for analysis. What's more, they are typical. You will encounter the same or similar ambiguities in many a moral argument, on many a topic.

THE PRINCIPLE OF CHARITY

The norm to follow in resolving ambiguities is known as the "Principle of Charity," since it enjoins giving an argument the benefit of any doubt. The name suggests a religious or ethical maxim. And indeed the principle takes that form too. "It must be presupposed," wrote Ignatius of Loyola, the Jesuit founder, "that every Christian must be more ready to excuse the proposition of another than to condemn it; and if he cannot save it, let him inquire how he understands it." Let him imagine viable interpretations, possible justifications, unstated grounds, apter formulations. Let him do everything he can to save another's argument and make it succeed. In this respect, too, let him treat his neighbor as he would wish to be treated himself.

However, the Principle of Charity is a practical as well as a moral precept. What it prescribes is something more than a benevolent attitude or friendlier way of treating other people; it is, in addition, a surer way to the truth. For suppose that whenever a person failed to make his meaning perfectly clear, we adopted the weaker of two readings or formulations or made no effort to divine unstated premises or connections. Suppose we consistently gave not the most benign interpretation but the least favorable, so as to invalidate the argument. What inference could we then draw from our refutation, concerning the truth of the argument's conclusion? Not that the conclusion was false. Not that no variant of the argument could prove it. Only that this weaker version does not. But a stronger version might. A stronger one might lead us to a valid answer, or at least to a likelier one than contrary arguments show. And if it didn't, we would know that *no* plausible rendering of the argument succeeds any better. For we would have tested the strongest version and found it wanting. In either eventuality, therefore—whether the argument succeeded or whether it failed—we would learn more about the debated issue by being charitable than by being uncharitable. And supposedly that is the aim of argument evaluation: to discover the truth, not to refute an opponent, by fair means or foul.

This clear verdict in favor of charity brings immediate practical advantages. For it frees us from many a quandary. Should we state the conclusion this way or that? Should we interpret a premise thus or so? Should we suppose this or that unstated premise underlying the inference? Each time the answer is the same: "Choose the alternative that strengthens the case. Do unto others' arguments as you would have them do unto yours. Show the other person the same good will and understanding that you would like to be shown in turn."

ILLUSTRATIONS

An argument from chapter 3's first exercise provides a simple illustration: "Since smoking harms the smoker, and the smoke annoys others, smoking is wrong." You may not notice any unclarity here, but were you to evaluate the argument, an important ambiguity would likely catch your eye. The smoke from smoking does not always annoy others; often there are no others around to be annoyed. So how, you might wonder, can annoyance on some occasions show that smoking is wrong on all occasions? Well, is that what the conclusion asserts? Does it condemn all smoking regardless of circumstances, or does it perhaps make the more moderate claim that smoking is, in general, a bad habit, though individual acts of smoking may sometimes be all right?

A more fully developed argument might leave no doubt about the author's meaning. If, however, we had no more than this one sentence to go by, we could have recourse to the Principle of Charity to resolve the uncertainty. Which reading makes better sense of the argument? Which interpretation strengthens it? Clearly the one that connects the conclusion more strongly with the premises. The annoyance smoke *sometimes* causes could not show that smoking is *always* wrong, whereas even frequent annoyance to others would be a further reason for disapproving the *habit*, if not every individual act. The latter reading, then, is the one we should prefer.

This benign interpretation is not unrealistically charitable. We are not playing make-believe in suggesting it. For the possibility of smoking alone (in one's room, on a walk, out in the woods) and the possibility of others' not being annoyed even if present (since they too are smoking, or the room is well ventilated, or they find the aroma of a pipe rather pleasant) are not little-known facts likely to have escaped the arguer's notice. Supposedly he or she knows them as well as you or I. And supposedly he or she recognizes as readily as we do the difficulty of deriving a universal condemnation from just occasional, though frequent, annoyance. So why take the conclusion in that less-supported, easily criticized sense? Why suppose that it censures every single puff?

Once we have picked a sense for the conclusion, we can complete the first part of the four-part process outlined in chapter 3. For notice that that is where we still are, at the very start of the procedure. We have not yet diagramed or evaluated the argument. We have not yet assessed the truth of the first premise, for instance, concerning harm to one's health, nor considered how much support that premise together with the second gives the conclusion. The Principle of Charity has required some initial weighing, it is true; but its purpose was simply to determine more exactly *what* argument to assess, more thoroughly and systematically, later on in the procedure. Shall we read the conclusion in the more vulnerable way or in the less vulnerable?

In this instance, for this argument, the Principle of Charity furnishes a solution, the ambiguity is removed, and we can carry on (diagraming, weighing the premises' truth, assessing the connection). Other times, however, the quandary remains, despite our best efforts. One interpretation fails one way, another fails another, and we are left on the horns of a dilemma. A typical illustration is the kind already cited: one reading makes a premise true, but destroys its relevance; another restores its relevance, but undermines its truth. There is nothing the Principle of Charity can then do to resolve the impasse, for no benign reading exists. Each alternative is equally fatal to the argument.

Suppose, for instance, that for purposes of simple illustration we make the argument on smoking read as follows: "Since the smoke annoys others, smoking is always wrong." The sense of the conclusion is now clearer. But with it clarified this way rather than the other, we may wonder instead about the premise. If the premise means "the smoke *always* annoys others," it connects with the conclusion but is evidently false. If it means "the smoke *often* annoys others," it is true but does not connect with the conclusion. How does the annoyance *sometimes* caused show that it is *always* wrong to smoke? What about some solitary fisherman, say, off in the middle of Lake Michigan?

In such an instance the Principle of Charity cannot help. No preferable reading can be found. One sense weakens the argument one way; the other weakens it another way, and equally. This does not mean, however, that the principle, or analysis, has failed. Quite the contrary. Analysis has done its job and succeeded. It has succeeded so well that no further step may be necessary. If the problematic premise is crucial to the argument, as here, further evaluation would be superfluous. The argument's secret has been spotted, its weakness laid bare: it trades on a basic ambiguity.

Practically, and for purposes of this course, this means that when one reading looks somewhat stronger than another, you can go ahead and write a streamlined version of the argument, employing that sense; draw up a diagram; and proceed to evaluation. The procedure can be carried to term. When, however, each alternative reading proves equally disastrous for the argument, your work is done. Write up the dilemma and dismiss the argument as worthless.

EXERCISE 1

Here is a real-life argument, now, with multiple ambiguities (listed below) to practice on. Read each premise first in one sense, then in the other, and ask: Does one interpretation do better by the argument than the other? If so, why? If not, why not? Would some third, unmentioned sense perhaps do better?

"The democratic philosophy is based on man's ability to reason and decide for himself his own best interests, on his educability, and on his conscience. Obviously, censorship denies each one of these. Regardless of the issue of what is true and what is false, of what is dangerous or what may be considered obscene, completely free expression is invaluable for progress. Censorship

—*any* censorship—can not be justified in a democracy if we really believe in man's freedom to choose for himself, in man's God-given right to motivation by his own conscience, and, finally, in the ability of man to learn only when he is given an opportunity to learn by seeing all knowledge spread out before him."

(Eli M. Oboler, "The Freedom to Choose," *Intellect*, January 1975, pp. 263–64)

Conclusion: Censorship is always wrong.

One Key Premise: Man (i.e., any person, male or female) can learn only when all knowledge is spread out before him.

Problematic Expression: "all knowledge."
One Sense: all opinions of what is the case.
Another Sense: all true opinions.

A Second Key Premise: Man has a right to motivation by his own conscience.

Problematic Expression: "motivation by his own conscience."
One Sense: form his own opinion.
Another Sense: always act on his own opinion.

A Third Key Premise: Man is free to choose for himself.

Problematic Expression: "is free."
One Sense: has the ability to choose (cf. "man's ability to . . . decide for himself").
Another Sense: always has the right to choose.

A FATAL CONFIGURATION

The preceding samples have illustrated ambiguity in the conclusion and ambiguity in a premise. They have illustrated resolvable ambiguity and irresolvable ambiguity. And they have suggested, in a preliminary way, their importance. So the practical question becomes: How can such ambiguities be spotted? Do they signal their presence, in premise or conclusion, by some telltale trait? So might some procedural rule be stated, saying when and where to look closer? No, that is not possible. The ambiguities are too varied and too well concealed. But practice can help. Sample analyses like those above and those to follow can sharpen your perceptions in two important ways.

First, the more such traps you are shown, the more conscious you will be of their existence, and the more wary of falling into them. Alerted to the perils of ambiguity, you will be less easily duped by your own fuzzy arguments or by those of others. Each new example will drive the lesson home: before rushing to a conclusion, be sure you grasp the argument; before assessing the argument's soundness, make sure you catch its drift. How, precisely, should it be understood?

Second, the more traps you are shown, the more conscious you will become not only of their existence and their multiplicity but also of their typical forms. You will get acquainted, so to speak, with the Malay mancatcher, the Burmese tiger pit, and various other well-concealed disasters awaiting the unwary. You will become familiar, in particular, with the most prevalent pitfall of all, exemplified by the following argument.

On the issue of executive responsibility, Milton Friedman, the well-known economist, has written as follows:

> What does it mean to say that the corporate executive has a 'social responsibility' in his capacity as businessman? If this statement is not pure rhetoric, it must mean that he is to act in some way that is not in the interest of his employers. For example, that he is to refrain from increasing the price of the product in order to contribute to the social objective of preventing inflation, even though a price increase would be in the best interests of the corporation. Or that he is to make expenditures on reducing pollution beyond the amount that is in the best interests of the corporation or that is required by law in order to contribute to the social objective of improving the environment. Or that, at the expense of corporate profits, he is to hire 'hardcore' unemployed instead of better-qualified

available workmen to contribute to the social objective of reducing poverty.

In each of these cases, the corporate executive would be spending someone else's money for a general social interest. Insofar as his actions in accord with his 'social responsibility' reduce returns to stockholders, he is spending their money. Insofar as his actions raise the price to customers, he is spending the customers' money. Insofar as his actions lower the wages of some employees, he is spending their money.[1]

I know no reason to suppose that Friedman was insincere or meant to trick his readers. Yet a crucial ambiguity lurks in every sentence of his concluding argument. In what sense would it be "their" money—the stockholders', customers', or employees'—that the executive spent? In the sense that they *would* receive it if he didn't spend it, or in the sense that they *should* receive it? The first interpretation makes the premises true enough (at least collectively) but disconnects them from the conclusion. Granted, the stockholders, customers, and/or employees would get more if the executive spent less, but what does that have to do with the question whether they *should* get more? The second interpretation restores the connection with the conclusion but proceeds to beg the question. Granted once again, if they should get the money he shouldn't spend it, but *should* they get it? *Is* that the proper distribution? Read this second way, the argument simply assumes the answer to the very question at issue: Where should the money go?

Thus the argument is impaled, irremediably, on the horns of a dilemma. Take the word "their" in one sense (what they *should* receive) and it begs the question; take it in the other (what they *would* receive) and it is irrelevant to the question. In one interpretation there is no reason to consider the premises true; in the other there is no reason to consider them pertinent. And they can't be read both ways at once.

The particular pitfall exemplified by this sample is

so common that we had better take a closer, more systematic look at its structure. The argument just scrutinized and others below on widely varied topics reveal the following fatal configuration:

(1) *A premise may plausibly be read in either of two (or more) ways.*
For example, the assertion "The money is theirs" may be read either as stating what they would receive or as stating what they should receive.

(2) *One plausible sense is moral, the other not.*
In our illustration the assertion that the money is theirs may be taken to mean either that they should get it (the moral sense) or simply that they would get it (the nonmoral sense).

(3) *In one reading the premise's truth is problematic; in the other its connection with the conclusion is problematic.*
It is true, for example, that if less were spent on social responsibilities, more would go to consumers, employees, or stockholders; but it is not clear what this proves. It is evident, on the other hand, that if more should go to the latter, less should go to the former — the conclusion does follow; but the truth of the premises, so understood, remains to be established, for they beg the question at issue. *Do* the consumers, employees, or stockholders have a right to the money? *Is* that where it should go?

(4) *It is the moral sense that strengthens the connection but weakens the premise's truth, whereas the nonmoral sense strengthens its truth while weakening the connection.*
This is natural enough if you think about it. For the conclusion in a moral argument is a moral claim. And a premise will get you there more readily if it already makes the moral claim in question. If, on the other hand, it does not thus

anticipate the verdict, its truth will be less problematic but its probative force will be lost. The premises about "their" money, for example, no longer prove their point if they merely describe, whereas if they do more, and assert where the money should go, their truth becomes problematic. Where the money should go is what the debate is all about.

(5) *The argument draws its apparent strength from the conflation of both senses, that is, of the truer, nonmoral sense and the more probative, moral sense.*

Were someone to say in plain terms: "If less is spent on social responsibilities, more will go to consumers, employees, or stockholders, so that is where it should go," the premise would be strong but the connection would be shaky. Were someone to say in equally plain terms: "Consumers, employees, or stockholders have a right to the money that might be spent on social responsibilities, and therefore it should go to them," the connection would be sure but the premise far from evident, at least for anyone in need of proof that executives should ignore the claims of society at large. Let someone declare, however, in less plain terms: "The money is theirs, so they should receive it," and both the premise and the connection may now seem sure—provided the ambiguity of the word "theirs" goes undetected.

Here, then, its construction fully revealed, is the Malay mancatcher of moral reasoning, the Burmese tiger pit of ethical argumentation. The configuration is common, it is often difficult to spot, and it is usually fatal to an argument. Sometimes, as in Friedman's argument, both senses prove equally weak. Sometimes, as in some arguments below, one sense proves still weaker than the other. But in either case the argument's plausibility vanishes upon closer examination. So the more familiar you become with this configuration, the better. The following exercises do not presuppose such familiarity but aim to develop it. I shall therefore furnish some initial guidance, stating conclusions and pinpointing crucial ambiguities before leaving you on your own to determine how fatal the ambiguities are.

ARGUMENTS FOR ANALYSIS

In each of the arguments below: (1) Replace the problematic expression with one suggested sense, then with the other. In the first argument, for example, make the premise "To sell homework is *dishonest*" read "To sell homework is *deceptive*" (the first suggested sense for "dishonest"), then "To sell homework is *immorally deceptive*" (the second suggested sense for "dishonest"). (2) Assess each alternative reading for truth value and strength of connection. (3) Determine whether one reading does somewhat better than the other or whether each is equally damaging to the argument. Does one, for instance, weaken the connection, while the other undermines the premise's truth? Which does which? Would some other plausible interpretation of the problematic expression make the argument stronger?

All this evaluation might give the impression that the earlier method for evaluating arguments, proposed in chapter 3, has somehow fallen from favor and is being replaced by another. However, the explanation is the same as before. The recommended four-part procedure requires that we state premises and conclusions, clearly and precisely, at the start; only then are diagraming and evaluation possible. But we cannot state an argument's parts precisely until and unless we know their precise senses. And to determine their senses we may need to employ the Principle of Charity, as, for instance, in these present samples. Thus we are still at the initial, analytic stage of the four-part process; and the title for this section—"Arguments for *Analysis*"—is therefore appropriate.

1. SELLING HOMEWORK

"In this age of tax-chiseling, padded expense accounts and political pay-offs, it's a small wonder a kid would take to selling his homework. Someone should explain to the boy that it is admirable to help friends with their homework by showing them how to do it. But a person who sells 'help' is supporting dishonesty in them and behaving dishonestly himself."

(Ann Landers, quoted in Robert Baum, *Ethical Arguments for Analysis*, brief ed. [New York, 1975], p. 34)

Conclusion: It is wrong to sell homework.
Key Premise: To sell homework is dishonest.
Problematic Expression: "dishonest."
One Sense: deceptive.
Another Sense: immorally deceptive.

2. ORGAN TRANSPLANTS

"Surgeons have been successful in curing sick persons of physical and mental diseases by grafting on them parts of the organs of another person. . . . Are these transplantings permitted by the moral law? The larger number of moral theologians hold a negative opinion. According to them, the removal of organs or parts of organs from a healthy man is unlawful, because it would involve mutilation of a living individual, which is unlawful."

("Transplantation of Organs," in *Dictionary of Moral Theology*, ed. P. Palazzini [Westminster, Md., 1962], p. 1241)

Conclusion: Transplants are wrong.
Key Premise: They involve mutilation.
Problematic Expression: "mutilation."
One Sense: action depriving a person of a bodily organ or its use.
Another Sense: action wrongly depriving a person of a bodily organ or its use.

3. A-BOMBING

"No discussion of this question however incomplete can neglect the argument that the atomic bombs were used to bring about a quicker surrender of the Japs and thereby in the end save lives.

The plea is specious but unethical. The end does not justify the means. It is not permissible to do evil that good may come."
> ("Editorial Comment," *The Catholic World*, September 1945, p. 451)

Conclusion: It was wrong to bomb Hiroshima and Nagasaki.
Key Premise: It is not permissible to do evil that good may come.
Problematic Expression: "evil."
One Sense: moral evil.
Another Sense: nonmoral evil (destruction, loss of life, etc.).

4. LYING

"The essence of the evil of lying consists in the abuse of the faculty of speech, for the primary purpose of speech is to reveal what is in the mind, whereas, in lying, that purpose is frustrated in the very act of speech."
> (Henry Davis, *Moral and Pastoral Theology*, vol. 2 [London, 1958], p. 411)

Conclusion: Lying is wrong.
Key Premise: It frustrates the primary purpose of speech.
Problematic Expression: "primary purpose."
One Sense: the purpose speech should always serve.
Another Sense: the most important of the purposes it serves.

5. ABORTION

"The liberal asks, 'What has a zygote got that is valuable?' and the conservative answers, 'Nothing, but it's a human being, so it is wrong to abort it.' Then the conservative asks, 'What does a fetus lack that an infant has that is so valuable?' and the liberal answers, 'Nothing, but it's a fetus, not a human being, so it is all right to abort it.'"
> (Roger Wertheimer, "Understanding the Abortion Argument," *Philosophy and Public Affairs*, 1971, p. 85)

Problematic Expression (both times): "human being."
One Sense: a being possessing human traits (e.g., a human genetic code in the first argument, social awareness in the second).
Another Sense: a being endowed with human rights, including the right to life.

Arguments for Analysis 93

6. SMOKING

"The law of love involves three persons: God, our neighbor, ourselves. Smoking sins against all three:
   "Only God, according to moralists, has direct dominion over creation. We are only stewards of our bodies; by persistently injuring our bodies, we assume dominion over them, thereby displacing God."

(Yvonne Goulet, "It's a Sin to Smoke,"
U. S. Catholic, June 1973, p. 14)

Conclusion: Smoking is wrong.
Key Premise: Only God has direct dominion over creation.
Problematic Expression: "direct dominion over creation."
One Sense: the right, directly, to treat creatures as he pleases.
Another Sense: the right, directly, to treat creatures as is right.

7. ARTIFICIAL CONTRACEPTION

"Arguments proceeding within the framework of conventional natural-law theory always include the following incomplete syllogism: *Contraception is intrinsically immoral because by it one engaging in intercourse prevents his act from attaining its natural end.* This syllogism can be understood and completed in various ways. . . . The obvious way to expand the incomplete argument into a formally valid syllogism is the following.
Major: To prevent any human act from attaining its natural end is intrinsically immoral.
Minor: Contraception prevents sexual intercourse from attaining its natural end.
Conclusion: Contraception is intrinsically immoral."

(Germain Grisez, *Contraception and the Natural Law* [Milwaukee, 1964], p. 20)

Problematic Expression (in both premises): "its natural end."
One Sense: the end which it typically or frequently attains.
Another Sense: the end which it should always be allowed to attain.

8. SUICIDE

"There is what might be called a perilous 'moral irradiation' in letting the end justify the means in the question of suicide. If suicide is right for *any* reason, such as safeguarding national secrets, the way is open for permitting it in order to preserve honor or escape the intolerable pain of terminal cancer. The original concession made to fine motives becomes an opening wedge for a general assault on all the sanctities of life. The transition is easy from permissible suicide to legalized euthanasia and all the horrors of a political eugenics program such as the one Hitler imposed in the last monstrous years of the Third Reich."

("What About Suicide?" *America*, September 3, 1960, p. 591)

Conclusion: Suicide is always wrong.
Key Premise: The transition is easy from permissible suicide to impermissible.
Problematic Expression: "permissible suicide."
One Sense: suicide that *is* right for any reason.
Another Sense: suicide that is *thought* right for any reason (cf. "the original concession").

9. EXTRAMARITAL SEX

"We shall now pose a more complicated problem in the sphere of interpersonal relationship. Bob and Betty have been dating one another for about a year. For some time their relationship had been warmly cordial, with only an occasional kiss to remind one another that they were, as some folk quaintly put it, of 'opposite sexes.' However, more recently Bob and Betty had been pressing cordiality to somewhat perilous limits. Tonight they had attended a church dance and were now ostensibly on the way home.

"But the night was yet young, and Bob's heart being full of love for Betty, he decided to park at the lake shore. Betty found herself in immediate agreement with the idea, and as this ageless story goes, one thing led to another until Bob found himself demanding from Betty, in the name of an eternal love that knows no dying, and with the incoherence such situations invariably call forth, the ultimate gift she was able to give him.

"The new morality has been charged by its critics with being obsessed with such situations—and more than that, with encouraging a bland permissiveness in the area of sexual relationships. The new moralists have been forced to become highly defensive at this point. Their moral scheme, they have said, has to do with moral problems of every kind, from the simplest difficulties in personal relationships to the question of American involvement in South Vietnam. Bishop Robinson has protested that the new morality has become identified in the popular mind with an 'invitation to sexual licence,' with himself the author of it. . . .

"Robinson declares that love's gate is strict and narrow, its requirements infinitely deep and penetrating. It would be triflingly easy for Bob to ask, in his relation to Betty, 'Why shouldn't I?', and then answer, 'Because it's wrong,' or 'Because it's a sin.' It is far more demanding of one to ask, 'Do you love her?' or 'How *much* do you love her?' and then accept *'for himself* the decision that, if he doesn't, or doesn't very deeply, then his action is immoral, or, if he does, then he will respect her far too much to use her or take liberties with her. Chastity is the expression of charity—of caring, enough.'"

(Elton M. Eenigenberg, "How New Is the New Morality," in *The Situation Ethics Debate*, ed. Harvey Cox [Philadelphia, 1968], pp. 211–13; reprinted from *The Reformed Review*, March 1967)

Conclusion: Bob should not have intercourse with Betty.
Key Premise: "if he does [love her], then he will respect her far too much to use her."
Problematic Expression: "use her."
One Sense: satisfy his desire at her expense.
Another Sense: be governed in her regard by his desire.

PART TWO
Arguments and Issues

As the title of this second part suggests, in the following four chapters we shall now get down to cases. Emphasis can shift more fully, as it gradually did in part one, from the theory of moral reasoning to its practice, with specific moral arguments and issues in the forefront. Each chapter will open with a collection of arguments for analysis and evaluation, raising issues for personal reflection and discussion.

The arguments are gathered under theoretical-sounding headings: "Rival Approaches," "Universal Norms," "Rules of Preference," "Morality and Law." But this does not mean that they serve primarily to illustrate theoretical points. Rather, the clustering permits common Background Remarks to help with evaluation. The full process of analysis, evaluation, and personal argumentation introduced by chapter 3 cannot be carried through successfully for any argument, in any chapter, without addressing the theoretical issues treated in that chapter's Background Remarks.

Ideally, the fuller such background preparation is, the better; realistically, the simpler and more concise it is here, the better. The ability and interests of typical beginners, as I perceive them, suggest that theory be lightly dosed and attention center on concrete moral problems. The Background Remarks are therefore just that — mere remarks, mere stimuli for further reflection, not systematic, comprehensive treatments of their topics. Students who wish fuller acquaintance with the history and complexities of a given theme may consult the readings listed for that chapter. The treatments cited are all more thorough than mine, yet still on an introductory level. Instructors, of course, may also amplify my remarks, and can do so more readily than they could simplify an overcomplex discussion. They will find detailed suggestions on how to handle this part of the text in the Teacher's Guide for this book.

CHAPTER 5

Rival Approaches

At the beginning of this and subsequent chapters you will find, not a text to read, but a collection of "Arguments for Analysis and Evaluation" to choose from, then "Background Remarks" and "Further Reading" to help with evaluation, followed by a "Sample Analysis-Evaluation" (or "Sample Evaluation" in chapter 8's two parts) to illustrate concretely just how to proceed.

The reason for grouping together the arguments that follow, and for putting them here at the start of part two, can be grasped from chapter one's account of "framework questions." Some questions, it explained, are broader, others more narrow; some are decisive for more actions, others for fewer. Through their varied approaches to the topics they debate, the arguments in this opening collection draw attention to the broadest, most decisive questions of all. To opt for one or the other of the norms operative in these arguments is to trace a general framework for all subsequent moral discussion.

ARGUMENTS FOR ANALYSIS AND EVALUATION

1. TRUMAN'S DECISION TO USE THE ATOMIC BOMB

"On the second proposition, raised by the Interim Committee, a sharper consensus *did* emerge: that the bomb should be used as soon as possible against a major military target to force Japan promptly to her knees. . . . There was general revulsion within the committee, according to Secretary Stimson's recollections, against the idea of the mass slaughter that would result from bombing a populated center. But weighing against this was the prospect that the conventional ground, sea, and air attack then being waged against the fanatical Japanese would take at least another year and possibly as many as one million American and British casualties before victory could be achieved. One or maybe two well-placed bombs should, on the other hand, end the war in a matter of days.

"As for the alternative of a harmless demonstration, there were sound arguments against that, too. To make it effective, the event would have to be widely billed in advance so that the enemy could see the awesome blast, or at least know about it and be properly intimidated. But in the then current state of atomic science, there was no absolute assurance that this primitive device would go off as planned, or that the delivering plane and its crew would not be demolished in the process. Such an eventuality, it was reasoned, would be a mortal blow to the image of Allied invincibility and probably would encourage Japan to fight on more determinedly than ever. It could also, it was believed, cause the Russians, who had promised at the Yalta Conference to get into the war against Japan three months after Hitler was disposed of, to drag their feet.

"There was, after all, in that baleful, tortured summer of 1945, just one overriding objective to American world policy: to whip Japan and end the war in the shortest time with the least possible cost in men and money. The debate in the Interim Committee therefore resolved itself in forwarding to the President the following historic conclusion on what to do about the atomic bomb: '*We can propose no technical demonstration likely to bring an end to the war. We can see no acceptable alternative to direct military use.*'"

Cabell Phillips, The Truman Presidency
(New York, 1966), pp. 56–57.

2. HIROSHIMA AND NAGASAKI

"The bombs were dropped on Hiroshima and Nagasaki. The decision to use them on people was Mr. Truman's.

"For men to choose to kill the innocent as a means to their ends is always murder, and murder is one of the worst of human actions. . . . When I say that to choose to kill the innocent as a means to one's ends is murder, I am saying what would generally be accepted as correct. But I shall be asked for my definition of 'the innocent.' I will give it, but later. Here, it is not necessary; for with Hiroshima and Nagasaki we are not confronted with a borderline case. In the bombing of these cities it was certainly decided to kill the innocent as a means to an end. And a very large number of them, all at once, without warning, without the interstices of escape or the chance to take shelter, which existed even in the 'area bombings' of the German cities."

>   G.E.M. Anscombe, *The Collected Philosophical Papers of G.E.M. Anscombe*, vol. 3: *Ethics, Religion and Politics* (Minneapolis, 1981), p. 64.

3. EUTHANASIA

"It is the express command of God that we take no human life. On this point his command is quite explicit. Nor do either wording or context of 'Thou shall not kill!' allow of exceptions. Euthanasia, however, is the deliberate killing of a human being. Consequently, it is a deliberate transgression of an explicit command by God."

>   Eike-Henner W. Kluge, *The Practice of Death* (New Haven, 1975), p. 133 (not Kluge's own position).

4. WARFARE

"Such a pacifist rejects the notion of 'fighting in the spirit of love.' It is impossible to treat others *as* enemies without feeling that they *are* enemies. If we heed the injunction to love, we will not be able to kill the aggressor—even to save our life or that of others. The aggressor *also* is one of our 'loved ones'! In case of war, the enemy troops are draftees or 'volunteers'—as we ourselves would be.... They are citizen-soldiers too, sent out by their government to do its dirty work. As Muhammed Ali said when he declined military service during the Vietnam War, 'I ain't got nothing against them Congs!' The people we are asked to kill in warfare have no more claim to be hated than anyone else. Yet, if we love them, how can we kill them?"

>   Gerald Runkle, *Ethics: An Examination of Contemporary Moral Problems* (New York, 1982), p. 467.

5. SELF-DEFENSE

"A double effect may follow from the act of self-defense: first, saving one's life; second, killing one's attacker. Such an act, then, since it is done to save one's life, is not illicit; for it is natural to every thing to preserve its existence, so far as it can."

Thomas Aquinas, *Summa Theologica*,
II-II, q. 64, a. 7.

6. CONTRACEPTION

"What assumptions does the general argument based on nature rest on? Why is it wrong to impede insemination [through withdrawal]? Why must nature be the ultimate standard? . . . The basic assumptions of Aquinas are that natural coitus was instituted by God; that the order of nature here is distinguished from the rational order; that natural coitus as instituted by God should not be altered by man. . . . Violation of this natural order is an affront to God, though 'no other person is injured.'"

John T. Noonan, Jr., *Contraception: A History of Its Treatment by the Catholic Theologians and Canonists* (Cambridge, Mass., 1965), pp. 239–40.

7. HELPFULNESS

"A *fourth* [person] is himself flourishing, but he sees others who have to struggle with great hardships (and whom he could easily help); and he thinks 'What does it matter to me? Let every one be as happy as Heaven wills or as he can make himself; I won't deprive him of anything; I won't even envy him; only I have no wish to contribute anything to his well-being or to his support in distress!' Now admittedly if such an attitude were a universal law of nature, mankind could get on perfectly well — better no doubt than if everybody prates about sympathy and goodwill, and even takes pains, on occasion, to practise them, but on the other hand cheats where he can, traffics in human rights, or violates them in other ways. But although it is possible that a universal law of nature could subsist in harmony with this maxim, yet it is impossible to *will* that such a principle should hold everywhere as a law of nature. For a will which decided in this way would be in conflict with itself, since many a situation might arise in which the man needed love and sympathy from others, and in which, by such a law of nature sprung from his own will, he would rob himself of all hope of the help he wants for himself. . . . We must *be able to will* that a maxim of our action should become a universal law—this is the general canon for all moral judgement of action."

Immanuel Kant, *Groundwork of the Metaphysic of Morals*, tr. H. J. Paton (New York, 1964), pp. 90–91.

8. TRUTHFULNESS

"The duty of veracity appears to be independent of the institution of contract and to rest simply on the fact that the respect due to another as a rational creature forbids misinforming him, not only for evil ends, but even for good ones. In duping another by lying to him, you deprive him of the opportunity of exercising his judgment on the best evidence available to him. It is true that the activities of a lying busybody may sometimes bring about a desirable result; but they do it by refusing to those whom they manipulate the respect due to them."

Alan Donagan, *The Theory of Morality* (Chicago, 1977), p. 89.

BACKGROUND REMARKS

In 1956 it was announced that Oxford University would confer an honorary degree on Harry Truman. Elizabeth Anscombe, the author of our argument 2, objected strenuously. "If you do give this honour," she protested, "what Nero, what Jenghiz Kan, what Hitler, or what Stalin will not be honoured in the future?" On Truman's authority Japanese cities were burned to cinders. At his order Hiroshima and Nagasaki were obliterated. If he followed his conscience, then his conscience was corrupt.

In Anscombe's view "for men to choose to kill the innocent as a means to their ends is always murder," no matter how desirable and important the ends may appear. Notice the key words: "as a means to their ends." Noncombatants may be killed, she would concede, in the bombing of a factory or a port. Thousands may perish in an invasion. But their deaths are then side effects; they are not directly sought, as means to one's goals. In Hiroshima and Nagasaki on the contrary, she believes, the slaughter and destruction did serve as means: they were intended to bring about Japanese surrender without need of an invasion. This relation of means to end is what made the deed so immoral.

Truman might contest this analysis of his intention (for the targets were also military), or while admitting that his intention was as described, he might defend its legitimacy. It is licit and right, he might argue, to employ even such dreadful means if the stakes are high enough. Anscombe's veto is not valid.

Now, when views thus diverge theoretically and not just factually, how may the conflict be resolved? When verdicts clash because theories clash, how may the theories' respective merits be assessed? Much as in other areas of inquiry, I would say. In ethics as in physics, chemistry, astronomy, or the like, theories can be compared for their consistency and for their agreement with the clearest and surest of our immediate, concrete judgments.

To illustrate the interplay between concrete data and general principles, consider some famous paradigms in physics. Newton's laws of gravitation are based on such data as the movements of falling bodies and the orbits of the moon, and in turn permit us to predict other movements (a comet, an eclipse, a shell's trajectory). Einstein's principles agree with more data (e.g., the perihelion of Mercury's orbit as well as falling raindrops) and anticipate more. Observe light as it passes the sun, and as his principles predict, you will find it is slightly deflected. If, however, the theory failed in this instance—if we looked and detected no such deviation—that would count against acceptance of the theory, at least as it stands. It might be preferable to Newton's formulation but would itself need further refinement.

Ethical inquiry may proceed in like fashion. We can examine clear, uncontested cases, draw general principles from them, then apply the principles to contested cases, like those at the start of this chapter. If the principles successfully illumine them, they are confirmed; if they somehow prove inadequate, they need to be revised, and the nature of the failure may show what the revision should be.

A Sample Derivation

As a clear and certain starting point we might, for instance, take Bambrough's observation in chapter 2 that a child about to undergo surgery (say an appendectomy) should receive an anesthetic. There is no gainsaying that. Any moral premise used to disprove it would be less sure than what it was meant to disprove. For a similar reason no proof is needed or possible. No premise used to demonstrate the anesthetic's rightness would be more certain than what it served to demonstrate. Here then is a datum as simple and sure as the proverbial falling apple that, according to legend, set Newton to thinking new thoughts about bodies and their motion.

Let us then reflect on this sample to discover its secrets. As we might ask "Why does the apple fall?" so we may inquire "What makes administering the anesthetic right and withholding it wrong?" The concrete answer, in this particular instance, is clear enough: "The pain." The agony the child would otherwise endure is a bad thing, and therefore should be prevented; the pain's absence is a good thing, and therefore should be sought.

This simple illustration exemplifies the link between values and disvalues, generally, and right action. A value, being good, is something that ought to be: its existence is better than its nonexistence. And if it ought to be, then it ought to be produced, preserved, or increased, as occasion allows. A disvalue, on the other hand, is something whose nonexistence is better than its existence, and which therefore should be avoided, prevented, or diminished as occasion permits.

Thus, as reflection on an apple falling to earth might suggest the law that bodies attract one another, so reflection on this single sure duty suggests the general principle: "Good should be done, evil avoided." Morality, like love, is a "many-splendored thing." Whether the good in question be pleasure, piety, health, wealth, friendship, freedom, art, or understanding, it should be maximized. Whether the evil be poverty, pain, ignorance, conflict, disease, degradation, error, oppression, or mental anguish, it should be minimized.

In our natural mode of calculation, maximizing value and minimizing disvalue generally turn out to be equivalent. To maximize comfort is to minimize pain, to maximize joy is to minimize sadness, to maximize knowledge is to minimize ignorance, to maximize security is to minimize insecurity, to maximize beauty is to minimize ugliness, to maximize friendship is to minimize hatred, to maximize health is to minimize hunger and disease, to maximize reverence for God or man is to minimize contempt and disrespect. So we needn't work out any more complex formulation, in terms of the balance of good over evil or of evil over good. "Maximize value, minimize disvalue" will do well enough.

Not Just Consequences

To avoid a basic misunderstanding, however, it is necessary to note that values and disvalues may result from actions or may be present in the actions themselves. The act of administering an anesthetic, for example, may itself be painless; an act that furthers friendship may itself be friendly; an explanation that brings clarity may itself be clear; a dance, concert, reading, or song may itself be a thing of beauty and not just a cause of beauty (say through imitation) or of pleasant feelings.

To be consistent, then, the principle "Maximize value and minimize disvalue" must be rightly understood. The logic of the position just developed clearly requires that in assessing the actions' merits and demerits, actions themselves be considered along with their likely effects. The dictum says to do good and avoid evil; it does not say, "But you can forget about good and evil when they belong to the act itself." No, maximize value and minimize disvalue comprehensively. Weigh total option against total option — the act along with its outcome.

This distinction between an act's worth in itself and in its consequences can acquire crucial significance, say in an argument like Donagan's (argument 8) "that the respect due to another as a rational creature forbids misinforming him, not only for evil ends, but even for good ones," or in a similar argument of chapter 6 against violating a person's autonomy by revealing confidential information, even when the revelation might serve the person's own best interests. In these arguments the authors give greater weight to an aspect of the deed itself than to its likely outcome. Elsewhere the fairness or unfairness of an act may similarly be stressed in contrast with the benefit or harm that may result from it.

Application

With this clarification added, in favor of comprehensive value-reckoning, we can turn from the norm to its application. How can the abstract standard just established and explained be brought to bear on specific moral problems? How, for example, does it relate to the issue debated in arguments 1 and 2 concerning the bombing of Hiroshima and Nagasaki?

Reliable application of the norm, in this or any instance, requires four things, each of which may prove difficult:

First, it is necessary to envisage *all* the more promising alternatives. (Was there really no other option than bombing the cities, trying a harmless demonstration, or eventually invading Japan? Mightn't nonmilitary measures have been preferable — say dropping the demand of unconditional surrender, assuring the Emperor's safety, and showing genuine interest thereafter in negotiations?)

Second, it is necessary to note all the relevant values and disvalues in each alternative. (Truman, for instance, seems to have paid slight attention to the casualties the Japanese would have suffered in an invasion, and the devastation inflicted on their homeland, though these too, in addition to allied casualties, weighed heavily against that alternative.)

Third, it is necessary to gauge, as best we can, the relative weight of each value and disvalue in view of its likelihood, extent, and specific kind. Even the apparently simple evil of the child's prospective agony reveals these three aspects or dimensions. If our verdict in favor of an anesthetic is so sure and strong, it is because without it her pain would be certain (not just probable or possible), prolonged (not just momentary), and severe (not slight, or mere discomfort). Her welfare would be triply jeopardized. (As for Truman, doubtless he considered, for example: how *likely* surrender would be if he used the bomb, how likely an invasion would be if he didn't; how *extensive* the devastation and loss of lives would be in one case, how extensive in the other; how precious *lives* were in comparison with property, or Japanese lives in comparison with American.)

Fourth, once values and disvalues have been identified and weighed, the sum of advantages and disadvantages for each of the more promising alternatives must be compared with the sum for each of the others. How many and weighty are the pros and cons on one side, how many and weighty are those on the other? The procedure we naturally adopt (cf. appendix B) resembles adding different plus and minus numbers in several columns (the alternatives) and preferring the column with the largest positive sum (maximum good) or the smallest negative sum (minimum evil). (Truman, for example, weighing many, sure Japanese casualties if he used the bomb militarily, against still more numerous but less sure Allied casualties if he didn't, opted for the former as the lesser evil. Like his advisors, he saw "no acceptable alternative.")

A Sample Confrontation

Such calculations, you recall, Miss Anscombe judged illicit when they lead to a decision like Truman's. It does not matter how many thousands will otherwise perish, whether Allied or Japanese, nor how widespread the destruction may otherwise be: in her view the death of even a single noncombatant may not be used as a means to achieve the greatest good or prevent the worst calamity. The causal configuration is decisive. Only if the noncombatant's death were directly caused along with some commensurate good (the destruction of a factory, a port, a military headquarters, a national leader) would the killing be permissible.

Implicit in this verdict, it would seem, as in many others like it, is a general norm sometimes stated quite explicitly: an evil of any kind, it says, no matter how slight, may not be used as a means to a good, no matter how great. Weighing and balancing are then ruled out. Good should not be maximized; evil should not be minimized. The action is automatically immoral the moment good and evil are thus causally related, the evil as means and the good as desired result.

Here, then, is a sample confrontation with which to test our sample norm. We derived it from sure data, with apparent sureness. But how well does it stand up now in comparison with rival standards? Which of these two conflicting norms, for example, is sounder: the one that enjoins value-maximization on all occasions or the one that repeatedly forbids it whenever the causal connection works out wrong? Well, which position is more consistent? Which squares better with our surest concrete judgments?

For a clear answer we need look no further than our initial illustration of the child's operation. The surgeon's incision — the gaping wound, the flowing blood, the danger of infection — is an evil (not a moral evil, to be sure, but a bad thing); and it is incurred for the sake of a subsequent, greater good. According, then, to the ban on all evils-used-as-means his action should be immoral. Yet practically no one would judge it that way, including those who on occasion assert or invoke the ban. Their position, therefore, is not consistent; nor does it agree with the basic data any theory must conform to. Any norm that condemns a safe appendectomy that will save a child's life is mistaken. *Seriously* mistaken.

In countless cases people use evils as means to good ends (they spank newborn babies to make them give a gasping cry, destroy fine woodlands to grow crops, kill living creatures to eat them, tell falsehoods to spare anguish, use bitters on the breast to wean, scold to reform, punish to deter, and so forth) without their actions being condemned on that account. It is the balance of good over evil that counts, not the relation of means and end. So our norm meets this first challenge quite convincingly. Others, however, await it.

Other Rivals

In this chapter's eight arguments for analysis and evaluation, only the first does value-balancing. Each of the others adopts a somewhat different approach. Anscombe, as we have seen, stresses causal relationships and bans an instrumental evil. The euthanasia argument appeals to God's command, the pacifist argument to love, the self-defense argument to natural inclinations, the contraception argument to "nature" and what is "natural." For Kant the decisive consideration is universalizability. Can I will that my maxim become a universal law? Can I will that everyone adopt it? Or would the attempt land me in some sort of contradiction, either with the laws of logic or with my own basic desires? In the eighth argument, finally, Donagan relies on a principle adapted from Kant: "Act always so that you respect every human being, yourself or another, as being a rational creature." This principle, he claims, rules out false statements made to mature, sane people. ("For benevolent purposes," he concedes, "it is sometimes permissible to dupe children, madmen, and those whose minds have been impaired by age or illness.")

A first critical query might be whether Donagan's principle does in fact carry this implication. Has it been rightly applied in this case? If so, is the principle itself sound? How well does it compare with the norm just advanced, of maximizing good and minimizing evil? Do the two standards—one centering on persons, the other on values—truly conflict? If they do, which is preferable? Which is more consistent, which more in keeping with our surest concrete verdicts? Such are the questions that can and should be asked for any of the arguments from 2 to 8.

FURTHER READING

Tom L. Beauchamp, *Philosophical Ethics: An Introduction to Moral Philosophy* (New York, 1982), chapters 3 and 4.

Richard B. Brandt, *Value and Obligation: Systematic Readings in Ethics* (New York, 1961), chapter 2 ("Which Acts Are Right?").

William K. Frankena, *Ethics*, 2d ed. (Englewood Cliffs, 1973), chapters 2 and 3.

Victor Grassian, *Moral Reasoning: Ethical Theory and Some Contemporary Moral Problems* (Englewood Cliffs, 1981), chapter 2 ("Theories of Normative Ethics").

Garth Hallett, *Christian Moral Reasoning: An Analytic Guide* (Notre Dame, 1983), chapters 4 to 6.

Gerald Runkle, *Ethics: An Examination of Contemporary Moral Problems* (New York, 1982), chapter 1 ("Ethics").

SAMPLE ANALYSIS-EVALUATION: #5 (SELF-DEFENSE)

1. Streamlined Version:

(1) All things are endowed by their creator with a tendency to preserve their existence, so far as they can. ("Natural" is an ambiguous expression. This seemed the strongest reading.)

(C) Therefore it is usually licit to kill one's attacker in order to save one's life. (With "always" rather than "usually" the conclusion would be still more difficult to support.)

2. Diagram:

①
│
Ⓒ

3. Evaluation of the Premise:

One thinks of radioactive substances, stars that eventually burn themselves out, volcanoes that naturally blow up, lemmings that periodically rush into the sea, the suicidal mating of certain insects, and so on. The premise's claim seems excessive.

4. Evaluation of the Connection:

From the alleged fact that all things have the tendency, we could infer that human beings have it. And from the fact that it comes from God, we might perhaps infer that acting on the tendency is generally a good thing (though a post-Darwinian view of creation might cast some doubt even on that). We could not however infer that acting on it in these particular circumstances, in this manner (taking an attacker's life so as to save one's own), is usually desirable and licit. That conclusion would require closer consideration of the values and disvalues typically at stake in such situations.

CHAPTER 6

Universal Norms

When people agree on the facts of a case but disagree on what should be done, they are led to discuss the specific norms that govern that type of act or situation. When they disagree about the specific norms, they are forced higher still, to reflect on what in general makes actions right or wrong. That is why, just now, the first chapter of part two started where it did, with comprehensive theories of morality. Such theories act as the court of last appeal. They set the standards that all precepts, all actions, must satisfy. Hence as we now turn our attention to the more specific norms in this chapter's arguments, we shall have some idea, thanks to that prior discussion, how to assess them.

According to the principle developed in chapter 5, moral rules, like particular acts, should somehow maximize value. But just how they should or may do so remains to be considered in this chapter. For the guidelines so far provided—with regard to alternatives, values, weights, and comparative totals—were tailored more for particular actions, such as bombing Hiroshima, than for universal norms, on adultery, war, abortion, informed consent, smoking, and the like, such as the following passages propose and argue for.

ARGUMENTS FOR ANALYSIS AND EVALUATION

1. ADULTERY

"In the realm of sexual behavior, there has been a commonly accepted rule, 'Thou shalt not commit adultery.' Reasons can be given for the authority of that rule, but the rule has relative autonomy by virtue of its long usage within the Christian community so that its members do not have to face every human relationship with a man or woman who is not their marriage partner as one that offers the moral possibility of adultery. Indeed, if for various reasons a relationship suggests that adultery might be committed, Christians begin with the rule. The weight of evidence and reflection clearly has to be such as to invalidate the application of the rule in that particular instance."

James Gustafson, *Theology and Christian Ethics* (Philadelphia, 1974), p. 116.

2. WAR

"If there is anything approximating a generally or widely held view among pacifists, it would perhaps be the following argument: War is, in no instance, the only effective means either to the prevention or reduction of serious wrongs or to the promotion of important but unafforded freedoms. Quite the contrary: we can achieve our desired social objectives better by entirely peaceful means. Certainly the most important of human values are sometimes threatened by invasions and other acts of aggression, but equally warlike responses only compound the difficulty by bringing greater measures of evil into the world. The existence of any military organization at all inevitably leads to atrocities. In short, war is counterproductive."

Tom L. Beauchamp, *Ethics and Public Policy* (Englewood Cliffs, 1975), pp. 174–75.

3. ABORTION

"'Respect life' is a rule whose habitual and exceptionless observance serves human societies better than any other rule that could be devised. . . . Nothing could weaken the rule more than unnecessary ('nontherapeutic') abortion. When mother and doctor can, for the flimsiest of reasons, terminate a life at any time during the first six months of its existence, the rule is weakened and our sensibilities are brutalized. We are thus prepared to compromise the rule in other cases."

Gerald Runkle, *Ethics: An Examination of Contemporary Moral Problems* (New York, 1982), p. 135 (not proposed as his view).

4. INFORMED CONSENT

"Precisely because there are unknown future benefits and precisely because the results of the experimentation may be believed to be so important as to be overriding, this rule governing medical experimentation upon human beings is needed to ensure that for the sake of those consequences no man shall be degraded and treated as a thing or as an animal in order that good may come of it. In this age of research medicine it is not only that medical benefits are attained by research but also that a man rises to the top in medicine by the success and significance of his research. The likelihood that a researcher would make a mistake in departing from a generally valuable rule of medical practice because he is biased toward the research benefits of permitting an 'exception' is exceedingly great. In such a seriously important moral matter, this should be enough to rebut a policy of being open to future possible exceptions to this canon of medical ethics."

Paul Ramsey, *The Patient as Person* (New Haven, 1970), pp. 8–9.

5. SMOKING

"The law of love involves three persons: God, our neighbor, ourselves. Smoking sins against all three:

"Only God, according to moralists, has direct dominion over creation. We are only stewards of our bodies; by persistently injuring our bodies, we assume dominion over them, thereby displacing God.

"We offend ourselves by smoking in that 1) we curtail our ability to function at peak efficiency (according to the same government report mentioned earlier, 'clinical studies involving healthy young men have shown that cigarette smoking impairs exercise performance especially for many types of athletic events and activities involving maximal work capacity'); 2) Smokers further offend themselves by increasing seven-fold their susceptibility to lung cancer and to other respiratory and cardio-vascular disease (Surgeon General's report).

"Smokers violate love of neighbor by 1) causing discomfort to others by polluting shared air; 2) causing physical damage to those with allergies or other respiratory ailments; 3) endangering the lives of unborn children they may be carrying; 4) endangering the financial and emotional security of those who depend upon them; 5) giving bad example to children and young people who may be influenced to smoke."

      Yvonne Goulet, "It's a Sin to Smoke," *U.S. Catholic*,
                   June 1973, pp. 14–15.

6. FAMILY HEAD

"In Christian marriage the man is said to be the 'head.' Two questions obviously arise here. (1) Why should there be a head at all — why not equality? (2) Why should it be the man?

"(1) The need for some head follows from the idea that marriage is permanent. Of course, as long as the husband and wife are agreed, no question of a head need arise; and we may hope that this will be the normal state of affairs in a Christian marriage. But when there is a real disagreement, what is to happen? Talk it over, of course; but I am assuming they've done that and still failed to reach agreement. What do they do next? They can't decide by a majority vote, for in a council of two there can be no majority. Surely, only one or other of two things *can* happen: either they must separate and go their own ways or else one or other of them must have a casting vote. If marriage is permanent, one or other party must, in the last resort, have the power of deciding the family policy. You can't have a permanent association without a constitution.

"(2) If there must be a head, why the man? Well, firstly, is there any very serious wish that it should be the woman? As I have said, I'm not married myself, but as far as I can see, even a woman who wants to be the head of her own house does not usually admire the same state of things when she finds it going on next door. She is much more likely to say 'Poor Mr. X! Why he allows that appalling woman to boss him about the way she does is more than I can imagine.' I don't think she is even very flattered if anyone mentions the fact of her *own* 'headship.' There must be something unnatural about the rule of wives over husbands, because the wives themselves are half ashamed of it and despise the husbands whom they rule. But there is also another reason; and here I speak quite frankly as a bachelor, because it is a reason you can see from outside even better than from inside. The relations of the family to the outer world — what might be called its foreign policy—must depend, in the last resort, upon the man, because he always ought to be, and usually is, much more just to the outsiders. A woman is primarily fighting for her own children and husband against the rest of the world. Naturally, almost, in a sense, rightly, their claims override, for her, all other claims. She is the special trustee of their interests. The function of the husband is to see that this natural preference of hers isn't given its head. He has the last word in order to protect other people from the intense family patriotism of the wife."

C. S. Lewis, *Christian Behaviour* (New York, 1943), pp. 35–37.

7. DIVORCE

"It is true that, in not a few instances, a man or a woman finds himself or herself joined perpetually in wedlock to a partner who is gravely objectionable. Habitual drunkenness, cruelty, a lascivious way of living, glaring incompatibility of temperaments—these are some of the reasons that can cause the ruin of marriages that began happily. In such cases as these, where it is entirely unreasonable to expect that the innocent party remain with the offending spouse, should there not be some remedy which would allow the victim of such an unfortunate circumstance to start his matrimonial life anew? Should not perfect [that is, complete] divorces be permitted in such exceptional and worthy cases? The answer is an unequivocal no. Because of the indissolubility of marriage many guiltless persons will, it is true, suffer, and suffer greatly. The welfare of the individual, however, should be subservient to the general good of society. A course of action which is best for the community must be favored, even though because of it great hardship is visited on some few. It is for this reason that perfect divorce is in all circumstances prohibited by the natural law. It is necessary for the good of society to forbid, without exception, perfect divorce. The reason that no exception may ever be permitted is that, if there were a possibility of obtaining a divorce even for a very serious reason, the parties could at will see to it, by directly procuring that reason, that it was verified in their case. If, for example, extreme cruelty were considered sufficient grounds for divorce, a husband who had grown tired of his wife could indulge in such cruelty with the

view to winning a perfect divorce as the reward for his brutality. Once exceptions to the rule of indissolubility were allowed, the opening wedge would inevitably lead to general abuse."
Edwin Healy, *Marriage Guidance*
(Chicago, 1948), p. 152.

8. CONFIDENTIALITY

"To respect autonomous agents is to recognize with due appreciation their own considered value judgments and outlooks even when it is believed that their judgments are mistaken. To respect them in this way is to acknowledge their right to their own views and the permissibility of their actions based on such beliefs. . . . Where competent adults are involved, breaches of confidentiality to protect the patient from himself usually involve a violation of autonomy, and therefore are difficult to justify. Suppose that a physician has to decide whether to disclose to a thirty-year-old woman's parents that their daughter's marriage is in trouble and that this is the cause of a 'nervous condition' which has resulted in her hospitalization. She has asked him not to say anything to her parents, but he is convinced that her parents, who are also his patients, would help her recover. The alleged benefit to the patient is not of sufficient magnitude or probability to warrant overriding autonomy and the rule of confidentiality in these circumstances. If the physician's efforts to convince the woman that she should tell her parents fail, he should maintain confidentiality even if he believes it is not in the patient's best interest."
Tom L. Beauchamp and James F. Childress,
Principles of Biomedical Ethics (New York, 1979),
pp. 58, 215.

BACKGROUND REMARKS

With the connivance of their officers, the men of an army unit were regularly treating themselves to one day of leave for every day of duty. Then a general visited their base. During his tour he asked one soldier pointblank what schedule they were following. The man replied, truthfully,

"One day on, one day off." Thereupon even their weekend leave was canceled.

That soldier was put in a tight spot. A truthful answer was likely to make him unpopular with the troops, perhaps unhealthily so — and did, to judge from the irate remarks of the man I heard recount the incident. On the other hand, things might have gone still harder for him had he lied to the general and had the truth then come out. In any case he had no time to reflect and weigh the pros and cons; he had to reply straight off. And even had he been able to pause without giving himself and his unit away, he might have found it difficult to reach a verdict, even from a personal, self-serving point of view. And a dispassionate appraisal of possible benefits and drawbacks for the unit, the army, and the nation as a whole would have proved still more difficult. So he needed a reliable rule to go by.

A traditional candidate has been "Never tell a lie." Once accept a rule like that and the problem would seem to be solved. If the general asks his question, you don't hesitate or calculate, you tell him. If your wife asks where you have been, you tell her. If your boss asks how much the trip really cost, you tell him. Life is simplified. And yet — if a journalist, a competitor, a plotter, a criminal, a lunatic, an enemy interrogator puts you similarly on the spot, do you tell him or her too? Do you "tell it as it is," regardless of who asks what, when, why, in what circumstances? "Never" starts to look like a dangerous word. Yet without it, what becomes of the solution? Aren't we back where we started, trying to figure out on the spur of the moment how much truth to tell to whom on what occasion?

When and why and to what extent we may rely on universal norms — how seriously we should take their "never" or "always" — is a much-debated question in contemporary ethics, one relevant to the arguments of this chapter. Is adultery always wrong (argument 1) or war (argument 2) or nontherapeutic abortion (argument 3) or medical experimentation without informed consent (argument 4) or smoking (argument 5) or divorce and remarriage (argument 7) or violating confidentiality even to protect adult patients against themselves (argument 8)? Should a family always have a head and should it always be the husband (argument 6)?

In each instance the answer depends on what kind the rule or precept is and how much, accordingly, it has going for it. Some useful distinctions between different kinds of rule are the following four, which can serve as a sort of checklist in sizing up a given norm.

(1) Analytic or synthetic

Compare the two statements "All black cats are black" and "All cats are black." The first statement cannot go wrong; the second not only can but does. For in the first the predicate, "are black," simply repeats part of what the subject, "all black cats," already says, and it is therefore inconceivable that anything which satisfied the subject description would not satisfy the predicate description too, whereas there is no such necessary link between the subject and predicate of "All cats are black." It is perfectly conceivable that some animal should be a cat but not be black.

In this pair of statements the contrast is evident; in others it is less obvious. Compare for instance "All rectangles have sides" with "All rectangles are squares." Once again the first statement cannot go wrong, whereas the second statement can and does. For the subject notion, "rectangles," when unpacked, reveals the predicate notion "have sides" already present in it but not the predicate notion "squares." Hence it is inconceivable that anything would satisfy the description "rectangle" and not the description "has sides," whereas it is perfectly conceivable that some figure would satisfy the description "rectangle" and not the description "square."

Statements like "All black cats are black" and "All rectangles have sides" are called "analytic," no doubt because analysis reveals the predicate present in the subject. Statements like "All cats are black" and "All rectangles are squares" are called "synthetic," no doubt because they "put together" two distinct notions rather than simply repeat a notion expressed by the subject term. Analytic statements are always true, by virtue of their terms' mere definitions, but are therefore empty: "All black cats are black" tells us nothing about the color of any actual cat; "All rectangles have sides" tells us nothing about the shape of any actual rectangle. Synthetic statements, on the other hand, are not empty, but neither are they necessarily true: it would be an interesting fact, if true, that all cats are black or all rectangles are squares. It happens, however, to be false.

Now this same contrast, between analytic and synthetic, holds for moral propositions as for others. Thus if, for instance, "Lying is always wrong" is taken to mean "Illegitimate falsehoods are always illegitimate," then, to be sure, it holds infallibly. For it thereby becomes analytic, that is, true by definition. What the subject expression already says, the predicate merely repeats. The norm is as foolproof as "All black cats are black." But also as vacuous. For it does not tell us which falsehoods are illegitimate, which not, and so provides no practical guidance. It leaves us on our own to figure out, as best we may, whether, for instance, we should answer the general truthfully when he asks the camp schedule.

Only synthetic norms solve our practical problems — that is, only ones whose moral predicate adds a new note to the description of the act. The description, say, is "All falsehoods," and the predicate adds "illegitimate." Or the description says "All willful falsehoods," and the predicate says "wrong." Now we know what to do. The general, for instance, will have to be told.

Or will he? Once the predicate differs from the subject, the link between them becomes problematic. What makes *all* such acts illegitimate? Why is it *always* wrong to tell a knowing falsehood? If valid, the precept does indeed give precious guidance. But *is* it valid? *Is* it true?

Similar doubts arise when, for example, we distinguish murder from killing, and stealing from taking another's property. If murder is wrongful killing, then of course we should never murder. If stealing is wrongful taking of property, then of course we should never steal. But is all *killing* wrong, or all killing of humans, or all killing of innocent humans? Is it always illicit to take another's goods, regardless of circumstances, regardless of the taker's need? Once the act is neutrally described and the predicate tacks on "right" or "wrong," problems may arise concerning the norm's validity. But not before. Not for an analytic norm. Hence the importance of distinguishing between the two varieties—synthetic and analytic.

(2) Positive or negative

Most ethicians would acknowledge that for many kinds of action, if not for all (as chapter 5 suggested), the weighing of pros and cons is legitimate and necessary. Once this need is recognized, the difference between *positive* precepts, that enjoin an action (e.g., "You should always do X"), and *negative* precepts, that condemn or prohibit an action (e.g., "You should never do X"), becomes crucial. To make good on the universal claim expressed by an "always" or "never," these precepts are forced in opposite directions: the positive toward ever greater vagueness and generality; the negative toward ever greater precision and narrowness.

Thus consider, for example, the following two tables of precepts, the first positive and the second negative:

Positive: Always repay your debts, in full, on time, in the manner agreed on.
Always repay your debts, in full, on time.
Always repay your debts, in full.
Always repay your debts.

Negative: Never kill.
Never kill your wife.
Never torture your wife to death.
Never torture your wife to death while giving her to believe you hate her.

In both of these series legitimate exceptions grow progressively fewer, thanks to the mounting vagueness of the positive precepts and the increasing definiteness of the negative. To see that this is so, contrast the first formula in each lineup with the last. Many, varied reasons might excuse a person from repaying a debt in full, or on time, or in the exact manner agreed on, as the first positive formula dictates; but much more rarely would these or other reasons excuse a person from repaying the debt at all, at some time, to some extent, in some manner, as the final formula vaguely enjoins. Again, various grounds might be cited — capital punishment, just war, self-defense, etc. — for causing a person's death and thus contravening the first negative formula; but they would not justify killing one's wife, by torture, while making her think one hates her. Here in the second, negative sequence each added specification — wife, torture, hatred — makes an exception less likely, whereas in the first the fewer the specifications the fewer the exceptions.

Notice, though, that the positive series does not in fact succeed, even at the end, in eliminating all likely exceptions. It is easy to imagine reasons for not repaying a debt at all (the debtor, say, may be destitute, or in prison, or the creditor may have died). This failure of positive norms is typical, for reasons I shall not go into here. Negative precepts, on the other hand, may do better, thanks to the double tactic illustrated by our final sample: the narrowing of the class of forbidden actions, the piling of disvalue on dire disvalue (death, physical agony, mental anguish). This double tactic, however, has a further, corresponding effect: The resulting norm tends to be so obvious that we have no need of it (*of course* we should not treat our wives in that barbaric fashion) and so restricted that it offers little practical guidance (who ever considered torturing his wife to death while giving her to believe he hated her?). Thus truth and utility seem not to mix.

(3) Summary or supplementary

A rule might be some help, however, if we knew in advance that it held in at least the majority of cases. And if we knew it was valid for practically all, we would not need to puzzle much on most occasions but might just go ahead and follow the rule. If, for instance, nine times out of ten it is best to tell the truth, then the soldier, when put on the spot, will have statistics in his favor if he opts to tell the truth.

Reflecting further on an example like this, we see that a rule may have more in its favor than just statistics. It may do something more than summarize the results of case-by-case consideration. There may be supplementary reasons for adopting and following the rule, distinct from those that recommend the individual actions it enjoins. The contrast between the two sorts of reasons is tricky; so let me spell it out in this sample instance.

First, then, individual speech acts strengthen mutual confidence if they are truthful and weaken it if they are untruthful. They convey knowledge, if truthful; and falsehood, if untruthful. And the knowledge allows people to conduct their affairs more successfully, whereas the misinformation leads to unpleasant surprises. Such are the reasons that make truthfulness right and untruthfulness wrong in the majority of cases.

In addition there are reasons that recommend the rule of truthfulness as a rule, over and above the reasons that apply to individual acts. A good ethical norm may, for instance, serve as an aid to present decision. Take a situation which falls under some rule which I know to be valid in most situations. There may not be time or means for me to learn much more about the present situation than just that it does fall under the rule. (Consider the case of the soldier, forced to reply instantaneously.) The details of the case, even if I can discover them, may be too complex for me to handle. (Again, think of the soldier.) My handling of them, even if intellectually efficient, may easily be distorted by bias or self-interest. (Imagine the man's feelings and the pressures on him from both sides as the general — and the soldiers — awaited his reply.)

Obedience to the norm may also aid future decisions. By deciding, however uncorruptly, not to follow the rule on this occasion, I may weaken its hold on me in other situations where it clearly ought to be followed. (Having told the general a whopper to his face, I may take lesser lies in stride.) And even if I could be sure that I was in no such danger, I might help others into it by publicly breaking the rule. (A convenient fib on that occasion, especially if successful, might confirm many in their easy acceptance of lying, whereas telling the truth, despite the cost, might suggest a sterner standard.)

"No man is an island," unaccountable for others. No man is a continent, unshakably firm in himself. And in those many areas of life where interest and passion are strong, and the issues complex, and time and ability for constant calculation very limited, it may be well to do as William James suggested in chapter 1 and consign ourselves to the custody of some well-considered rules.

(4) Actual or possible

Further advantages of further kinds depend on whether a rule is just envisaged or actually in vogue. Suppose, for instance, that I think it a good idea to drive on the right side of the road and do so. No one, myself included, will derive much benefit from my adoption of that rule unless others — many others — accept and follow it too.

But once that condition is fulfilled (as of course it is in this country) and I am not alone, then conformity to the rule has clear advantages. I know what others will do, they know what I will do, and we can proceed on our way with relative assurance (until, for example, someone enters the freeway by an exit ramp).

So it is for many a social or moral norm. Given prevailing practice and present expectations, conformity has clear advantages:

> What would become of the institution of marriage if the marriage vow were taken to mean "I will remain faithful unto you until the situation appears to me to call for adultery"? Or if parental responsibility were interpreted to mean "We will care for you so long as circumstances seem to justify the policy"? The classical utilitarians with their emphasis upon "reliability, predictability, certainty" saw clearly enough that this would not do, and would not do precisely because it would be against the interests of all concerned. Hence it is an essential part of our concept of "duty" or "obligation" that we are, as we say, "bound" to act in accordance with them. This does not necessarily imply that there are no circumstances in which we may break our obligations or be freed from them, but it does imply that we are not entitled, insofar as we are bound by such obligations, to do "what love requires in this situation" if this means acting solely on a simple utilitarian calculus.[1]

Ways of life like those mentioned, woven by countless acts of obedience to the rules and unwoven by too numerous exceptions, may be more or less desirable in themselves. In this respect they may differ from driving on the right versus driving on the left. Monogamy, say, may be preferable to polygamy; marriage to free love; democratic rule to authoritarian; cooperative economies to competitive or conflictual; egalitarian societies to stratified; unified societies to splintered. If so, rule observance is doubly or triply recommended in each case: not only by the benefits of each one's observance, regardless of others'; not only by the "reliability, predictability, certainty" resulting from uniformity; but by the collective way of life maintained in this manner.

Summing Up

Many rules, like those of a game, we observe automatically, unthinkingly, unless special circumstances suggest and perhaps warrant a deviation. Do moral rules merit like fidelity? Do they perhaps hold more strictly still? Or should they on the contrary serve as mere rules of thumb, reminding us from time to time of what is often or generally the better thing to do?

The answer depends largely on the type of norm in question, and how many considerations, therefore, weigh in its favor, and how strongly. So to size up the credentials of any particular precept, for instance in an argument above, you can start by running through the following checklist:

(1) *Is the rule analytic or synthetic?*
   If analytic, it holds without fail but does not tell us specifically what to do; if synthetic, it does, but more fallibly.
(2) *Is it positive or negative?*
   If positive, its chances are better the less definite it is.
   If negative, its chances improve with narrowing, especially narrowing that adds dire disvalues to the description of the act.
(3) *Does it simply summarize individual verdicts, or is it backed by further benefits, say to present or future decision-making?*
   If the former, how strong are the statistics that support it?

If the latter, how weighty is that statistical evidence but also how numerous and telling are the added advantages?

(4) *Is the norm just a possibility or is it presently practiced?*
If the latter, individual observance may contribute to the certainty and predictability of social intercourse and may perpetuate an intrinsically desirable institution.

Once you have checked a norm by this list, you will be better able to judge the strength not only of the norm but also of the argument deployed in its defense.

FURTHER READING

Tom L. Beauchamp, *Philosophical Ethics: An Introduction to Moral Philosophy* (New York, 1982), pp. 86–97.

A. K. Bierman and James A. Gould, *Philosophy for a New Generation* (New York, 1970), pp. 169–87 ("Rules and Situations").

William Frankena, *Ethics*, 2d ed. (Englewood Cliffs, 1973), pp. 37–41.

John Hospers, *Human Conduct: Problems of Ethics*, 2d ed. (New York, 1982), chapter 6.

Daniel Maguire, *The Moral Choice* (New York, 1978), chapter 7 ("Consistency and Surprise").

Patrick H. Nowell-Smith, *Ethics* (Baltimore, 1964), chapter 16 ("The Purpose of Moral Rules").

Andrew G. Oldenquist, *Moral Philosophy: Text and Readings*, 2d ed. (Boston, 1978), chapters 3 and 4.

SAMPLE ANALYSIS-EVALUATION: #7 (DIVORCE)

1. *Streamlined Version:*

(1) If human legislation permitted complete divorce for any reason, married people could see to it that the reason was verified in their case.

(2) Thus any exceptions to the legal prohibition would inevitably lead to widespread abuse.
(3) But a course of action which is best for the community must be favored, even though because of it great hardship is visited on some few.
(C) It is therefore necessary to legally exclude complete divorce, without exception.

(This version results from applying the Principle of Charity to the conclusion, which in one interpretation would concern just divorce and its morality and in another interpretation would concern the legal prohibition of divorce. The words "perfect divorce is in all circumstances prohibited by the natural law" (regardless of human legislation) suggest the first reading; the words "It is necessary . . . to forbid, without exception, perfect divorce" suggest the other. I have chosen the second reading because only when taken in that sense does the conclusion receive any support from the premises. It would be absurd and improbable for couples to say: "If we fight, beat one another, become alcoholics, commit adultery, perpetrate crimes and go to jail, or the like, it will be all right; if we then divorce and remarry, we shall have done nothing wrong." But such immoral means might conceivably be used to get around human legislation.)

2. Diagram:

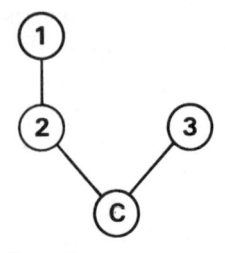

```
      1
      |
      2     3
       \   /
        C
```

3. Evaluation of the Premises:

Premise 1: Many reasons they could indeed verify at will (e.g., cruelty, neglect, infidelity), but not all that might be cited. Were insanity, for instance, made a sufficient reason for divorce, people might feign it but could not readily bring it about.

Premise 2: Since pretended infidelity, say, as well as actual would be an abuse, this premise is fairly strong. However, the premise (faithful to the original) speaks of "any exceptions," and it would not be easy, for example, to successfully feign insanity.

Premise 3: It might be objected that such a principle is not fair to the few. However, such unfairness results from practically any legislation, which must look to the common good.

It might also be objected that slight benefit for many would not justify great hardship for a few. However, if rightly understood, the premise seems true. The community referred to includes the few, and the premise therefore opts for an overall balance of good over harm. Rate the hardship to the few as high as you please, it implicitly says: if the good to be assured rates still higher, it should be preferred.

4. Evaluation of the Connection:

Here is the argument's major weakness. For the premises do not show that only a few would suffer hardship, or that the widespread abuses would cause comparable harm. After all, if a man is so tired of his wife that he is ready to beat her to obtain his release, the termination of such a marriage may be no great loss.

(So analyzed and evaluated, this argument might seem to belong in chapter 8, on morality and law. However, most authors and readers of natural-law arguments like this one have viewed them as being principally concerned with moral rules and not with legislation. So the appropriate place to begin discussion is in a chapter like the present, even if a benign interpretation then succeeds in shifting the argument to a context where its reasons make better sense.)

CHAPTER 7

Rules of Preference

Whether the decision to be made concerns bombing a city or applying an anesthetic, be sure it truly maximizes value and minimizes disvalue, chapter 5's norm prescribed. Choose the greater good; avoid the greater evil. But whose good should be maximized, whose evil minimized? Does that make any difference? Does it matter whether the child to be anesthetized is mine or somebody else's? Does it matter whether the lives to be saved are those of my fellow countrymen and the lives to be lost are those of foreigners? Do values and disvalues receive special weighting for me and mine, or should all human beings receive like consideration? Such are the questions, not yet considered, raised by the following arguments.

ARGUMENTS FOR ANALYSIS AND EVALUATION

1. AIDING THE NEEDY

"So there's plenty to be said in favor of keeping pets. But with all that in mind, I still say let's stop keeping pets. Not that a family should *exterminate* its pets. Very few could bring themselves to do that. To be practical, I am suggesting that if we do not now have a pet we should not acquire one; second, that if we now have a pet, we let it be our last one. I could never say that pets are bad. I am saying, let's give up this good thing—the ownership of a pet—in favor of a more imperative good.

"The purchase, the licensing, the inoculations and health care, the feeding and housing and training of a pet—and I chiefly mean the larger, longer-lived pets—cost time and money. Depending on the animal's size and activity, its special tastes and needs, and the standard of living we establish for it, the care of a pet can cost from a dollar a week to a dollar or more a day. I would not for a moment deny it is worth that.

"But facts outside the walls of our cozy home keep breaking in on our awareness. Though we do not see the famine-stricken people of India and Africa and South America, we can never quite forget that they are there. Now and then their faces are shown in the news, or in the begging ads of mission and relief organizations. Probably we send a donation whenever we can.

"But we do not, as a rule, feel a heavy personal responsibility for the afflicted and deprived for we are pretty thoroughly formed by the individualistic, competitive society we live in—a society whose unwritten rule is, 'I got mine, now let him get his.' The first dime we ever made for raking grass or shoveling snow was ours to spend in any way we chose. No one thought of questioning that. That attitude, formed before we had learned to think, usually prevails right through adulthood: 'I made my money. I can spend it any way I like.'

"But more and more we are reading that the people of the 'Third World' are resentful of us in the developed countries (with the United States far more developed than any of the others) for our grabbing up two-thirds of the world's wealth and living like kings while they scrounge all day for a yam and a bowl of rice—and die off at thirty-five or forty, provided they outlive the heavy scourge of infant mortality. . . .

"The money and the time we spend on pets is simply not our own to spend as we like in a time of widespread want and starvation. A missionary society advertises that for $33 a month they can give hospital care to a child suffering from *kwashiorkor*—the severe deficiency disease which is simply a starving for protein. Many a Boxer, Afghan, Irish Setter or Dalmatian requires at least that amount each month for his food and care. Doing without such a pet, and then *sending the money saved* to a creditable relief organization would mean saving a life—over the years, several human lives.

"Children not suffering from such a grave disease could be fed with half that amount—not on a diet like ours, but on plain, basic, life-sustaining food such as unpolished rice, soy meal, powdered milk, and an occasional guava or mango. It is not unreasonable to believe that the amount of money we spend on the average pet dog could keep a child alive in a region of great poverty. To give what we would spend on a cat might not feed a child, but it would probably pay for his medical care or basic schooling. The point needs no laboring. That is all that need be said."

John Mahoney, "Let's Stop Keeping Pets,"
U.S. Catholic, July 1973, pp. 14–15.
Quoted with permission of the editors.

2. HONESTY IN BUSINESS

"What about the Wall Street secretary who knows that her boss has decided to manipulate the price of a stock? Unless the Securities and Exchange Commission catches it, that's business as usual on Wall Street. 'It happens every day,' said Margie Albert, onetime brokerage-house secretary, now union organizer of office workers. 'Sometimes when they had a stock they knew was going to be good because they were going to push it to clients and make it good, they'd cut the secretaries in on it, arrange for the employees to buy some shares. Look, corporate life is shot through with corruption like this. What's a secretary supposed to do? Complain? She'd just lose her job. She's not the one who makes the decisions.'

"No, she isn't the one who makes the decisions. Yes, Ann Landers agrees, she would probably lose her job. And while it may be easy for me to risk someone else's job with my theories, I believe she should complain. If she is the Wall Street secretary, she should complain to the SEC for the sake of thousands of people who will be financially hurt (and you better believe that means the small investors). Complain for the sake of her dignity. They allow her to know because they think it's safe for her to know. She is, after all, just a secretary. She is identified with her function, not with the rational, judging, moral mind that is hers also. Secretary as Dictabelt, something you turn on when you want, turn off when you want, as devoid of a will of her own as a machine. Complain to be a human being."

B. J. Phillips, "The Secretary's Dilemma," Ms.,
March 1975, p. 68.

3. GRAFT

"I have a remarkable book called *From Far Formosa*, published in 1896. It's by a Scottish missionary named George L. MacKay. His account of the corruption that characterized Chinese society on Formosa in the late nineteenth century is fascinating. . . .

> I witnessed the execution of four soldiers condemned for burglary. One was on his knees, and in an instant the work was done. Three blows were required for the second. The head of the third was slowly sawed off with a long knife. The fourth was taken a quarter of a mile farther, and amid shouts and screams and many protestations of innocence he was subjected to torture and finally beheaded. The difference in the bribe made the difference in the execution.

"I think this episode illustrates in ghastly epitome what is wrong with bribery in general.

"We've heard otherwise respectable people say that, our own puritanism notwithstanding, there are societies that work well and smoothly thanks largely to graft, payola, esca, mordida, baksheesh, cumshaw, and so on. But there are lots of people at the bottom of the squeeze — people who for financial or ethical reasons can't put their share of golden grease into the works — and for them the squeeze can mean death, slow and painful, or, to bring it closer to home, twisting slowly, slowly in the wind."

Thomas H. Middleton, "Baksheesh, Cumshaw, and All That Grease," *Saturday Review*, July 9, 1977, p. 21.

4. FREER TRADE

"The world has seldom needed freer trade more than it does today; what trade freedom there is has seldom faced a greater threat. These simple truths are a text for governments in this year of dole queues and dear money, when politicians will be sorely tempted jointly to try to 'manage' (ie, distort) world trade. . . . When President Reagan slapped a limit on imported cars from Japan in 1981, West Germany became the last big open market for Japanese car companies. The Germans could not take the strain. Within a month they too had foisted a 'voluntary' agreement on Japan. Part of the capital invested in Nagoya's car factories — some of the most productive capital the world has ever had — was thus condemned to idleness. At the other end of the scale, consider a small developing country like Sri Lanka. Late into the industrialising ring and lacking political clout, it has had to turn away scores of textile companies eager to set up there. The domestic market is too small to support them, and Sri Lanka has used up all its textile quotas. Its growth is stunted, its young people denied the jobs and incomes that their education deserves."

"The First Trade Lesson," *The Economist*,
April 3-9, 1982, pp. 16, 18.

5. IMMIGRATION

"Even legal immigration, however, makes some public office-holders restive enough to argue that the national tradition of hospitality should be curtailed, if not abandoned. Governor Richard D. Lamm of Colorado, for example, made that genial view clear in 'America Needs Fewer Immigrants,' an essay he contributed to the op-ed page of The New York Times on July 12, 1981. As children or grandchildren of immigrants, the Governor wrote, we are blinded by our past myths and now 'we have to get our hearts in line with our heads and our myths in line with reality.' Once we have accomplished this bit of ideological chiropractic, we will see, Mr. Lamm thinks, that we must set strict limits on immigration, even if this seems selfish: 'Our immigration policy has to be designed in the interests of the United States.'"

John W. Donohue, "The Uneasy Immigration
Debate," *America*, March 20, 1982, p. 207.

6. DYING THAT OTHERS MAY LIVE

"Case 10: Captain Oates was a member of Robert Scott's expedition. As Oates and his companions were returning from the South Pole, the Captain had an accident and was disabled. The group was far from the depot which was their only source of food and shelter. It was obvious to all that if the others continued to help Oates, none would make it back safely. However, if Oates would detach himself from the group (an act which would ensure a quick death for him), the others would have a chance to return safely. What should Captain Oates do?

... In circumstances such as these, I want to argue, it is reasonable to say that Oates is morally required to detach himself from the group, in spite of the fact that such an act will lead to his death. Though such an act might well be described as heroic, it is still plausible to say that it is his duty and not a supererogatory act. . . . It is a crucial and morally relevant fact, I believe, that the same irreparable harm will come to Oates no matter what he does. Whether he leaves the group or not, he will soon die."

Terrance C. McConnell, "Moral Blackmail," *Ethics* 91 (1980–1981): 565.

7. GUARANTEED ANNUAL INCOME

"Given the present arrangement of our complex economic system, there will always be millions of persons unemployed, living on inadequate incomes, condemned to a life of degrading poverty.

"Some additional ingredient is needed in the economy to provide the assurance that everyone has the income they need to live in decency and dignity. This ingredient is guaranteed annual income.

"A Guaranteed Income program should include guaranteed employment for those who can work and guaranteed cash income for those who cannot or should not work.

"There are several elements in a guaranteed employment program, but the most important one is the concept of the government as the 'employer of last resort.' (In 1966, the President's Commission on Technology, Automation and Economic Progress recommended that the federal government constitute itself as 'employer of last resort.') This would place with the federal government the responsibility for assuring every employable person a job. It would include a matching and referral service, an effort to urge business and industry to hire, a stronger stimulation by providing funds to private businessmen or non-profit institutions to assist them in hiring needed employees, a work-training program to assist the unskilled or those with outmoded skills, and the establishment of public works programs to add to the number of jobs available."

Msgr. Lawrence J. Corcoran, "Let's Have a Guaranteed Annual Income," *U.S. Catholic*, September 1972, p. 12.

8. FOR FOREIGN AID

"There is no international power to check the economic power of the wealthy countries, to impose taxation, to redistribute property, to raise the bottom strata to a level of subsistence, to remedy the chronic malnutrition of the impoverished masses. What the rich have no right to, they are nonetheless able to retain. So Nagel must come to the same conclusion as Singer: 'While foreign aid is not the best method of dealing with radical inequality — being comparable to private charity on the local scene — it is the only method now available. It does not require a strongly egalitarian moral position to feel that the U.S., with a gross national product of a trillion dollars and a defense budget which is 9 percent of that, should be spending more than its current two-fifths of 1 percent of GNP on nonmilitary foreign aid, given the world as it is.'"

Gerald Runkle, Ethics: An Examination of Contemporary Moral Problems
(New York, 1982), p. 492.

9. AGAINST FOREIGN AID

"A grim expression of this point of view is that of the scientist Garrett Hardin, who compared the human situation to life on a lifeboat. There is not enough space (or food) on the lifeboat to rescue everyone. There is a point at which the survival of all is jeopardized by bringing more people aboard. 'The boat is swamped, and everyone drowns. Complete justice, complete catastrophe.' If food aid is given to the poorest countries, many of their people will survive, but this is only temporary, for the birth rate, far exceeding the death rate, will in time create food needs that the world will find impossible to meet. In terms of suffering, this would be a greater catastrophe than the ones that unaided countries now would face."

Runkle, ibid., pp. 494–95

BACKGROUND REMARKS

Consider an imaginary case: I, a great lover of pecan pie, have a whole pie at my disposal, which I can share or not share with someone equally keen on pecan pie. Five possibilities exist: I can keep the whole pie for myself; or keep the larger part; or divide the pie evenly with my companion; or give him the larger part; or let him have the whole thing. These solutions are mutually exclusive. Each conflicts with all the rest.

This simple paradigm can serve to represent both the issues and the possible solutions in the arguments above. For the issues, to start with, all have to do with the pie of human welfare and how it should be divided. We are led to consider, in turn:

> Should people keep the pets they enjoy, or use the money to feed the starving? (argument 1)
> Should the secretary risk her job for the sake of those who will be hurt by manipulations, or should she put her own interest before theirs? (argument 2)
> Should people gain personal advantage through graft, or forgo it for the sake of those who suffer in such a system? (argument 3)
> Should productivity and employment in one country be protected at the expense of other countries? (argument 4)
> Should the interests of those already in the U.S. take precedence over those of would-be immigrants? (argument 5)
> Should Captain Oates die so that his companions may live? (argument 6)
> Should some citizens sacrifice their surplus so that others may be assured a minimum? (argument 7)
> Should wealthy nations like the U.S. share more with destitute peoples? (arguments 8 and 9)

To options like these, various responses — of individuals, classes, or nations — are possible and likely. Our simple paradigm represents five. The five ways of dividing the pie suggest five "rules of preference" for dealing with such questions of distribution. Like the five ways, the rules are mutually exclusive and range from pure egoism to pure altruism.

The first, most egoistic norm would say: "Look out only for yourself and your own happiness, helping others only insofar as doing so furthers your own interests." Thus, if you would get more pleasure, without harm to your health, from eating the whole pie bit by bit, and if another's getting a piece would bring you no pleasure or profit, then eat it all. If the other person is a friend and you would receive more pleasure from sharing than from savoring the whole thing yourself, you should share. If the other person can be useful to you, you may win his favor by giving him a piece. The proper solution depends solely on how much benefit—for instance, how much pleasure—will likely come your way in each alternative. Self-interest is the sole criterion of how to behave.

In a society—a family, say, or an army at war—cooperative behavior is often in the best interests of all. The welfare of each individual being dependent on that of others, the sharing of burdens and benefits in ways perceived as "fair" or "just" repeatedly makes sense from even an egoistic viewpoint. Still, conflicts like those just noted, with regard to pets, immigration, foreign aid, free trade, and the like, are not all illusory. If one gets more, another may get less, and vice versa. And whenever interests do indeed clash, the first rule of preference ("Only my good counts") decides in one's own favor.

A more widely held rule still puts self first but is less purely egoistic. For it, too, charity begins at home. Thus in a one-on-one situation where it's my life or his, I should save my own. If no dividing or distributing is possible, but I get the job, the promotion, the house, the wife, the seat, the last chop on the plate or another person does, I should give myself the preference, once again, and take all. Where, however, benefits can be shared I should just take the bigger portion. Others' welfare and happiness count too, though not on a par with my own.

"I have shown you in all things that by working hard in this way we must help the weak, remembering the words that the Lord Jesus himself said, 'There is more happiness in giving than in receiving.'" — *Saint Paul*	"At the risk of displeasing innocent ears, I submit that egoism belongs to the essence of a noble soul, I mean the unalterable belief that to a being such as 'we,' other beings must naturally be in subjection, and have to sacrifice themselves to us." — *Friedrich Nietzsche*

Commoner still, it would seem, as an ethical norm or ideal, if not as a matter of actual practice, is a rule of parity, giving equal weight to others' good and one's own. If nine other people would enjoy the pie as much as I, I should divide it in ten pieces and give each of us an equal share. If I am needier than another, I should get more. If the other is needier, he or she should get more. And so forth. Thus in John Stuart Mill's utilitarianism, for example,

> the happiness which forms the utilitarian standard of what is right in conduct, is not the agent's own happiness, but that of all concerned. As between his own happiness and that of others, utilitarianism requires him to be as strictly impartial as a disinterested and benevolent spectator. In the golden rule of Jesus of Nazareth, we read the complete spirit of the ethics of utility. To do as you would be done by, and to love your neighbor as yourself, constitute the ideal perfection of utilitarian morality.[1]

The golden rule and Christian charity have often been understood still more altruistically. A fourth rule would reverse the second norm, above, and give preference to others rather than to oneself. A fifth rule goes further still and replaces the pure egoism of rule one with pure altruism. Thus many have agreed with Saint Basil that "The love which is according to Christ seeks not its own."[2] Each

> The five options in a nutshell:
>
> 1. self alone
> 2. self first
> 3. parity
> 4. others first
> 5. others alone

person, wrote Martin Luther, "should be guided in all his works by this thought and contemplate this one thing alone, that he may serve and benefit others in all that he does, considering nothing except the need and the advantage of his neighbor."[3] One's own good should not come into consideration save in relation to others'.

Jesus' self-sacrificing life and death are sometimes cited as evidence backing this norm. However, any form of altruism — whether self-preference, parity, other-preference, or self-forgetfulness — calls for frequent help to others and sacrifice of self, and may on occasion dictate the surrender even of life itself. For in a world inhabited by billions even if my good counts doubly or triply, I may easily get outvoted. (If fifty people, say, all want a taste of the pie, my slice may be slender.) In a world where so many individuals are so much worse off than I am, another's need may often outweigh mine. (If another is starving and I am well fed, I may rate a much smaller slice than he, or perhaps no slice at all.) In a world where the stakes are often so much higher than who will get more pie, coming out on the short end may mean, for example, losing my dog (argument 1), my job (argument 2), even my life (argument 6).

For most of the issues in this chapter's arguments even Mill's norm, favoring perfect parity, would likely entail some self-sacrifice. And how considerable the sacrifice might be appears when A. C. Ewing writes:

While the obligation to contribute something to charity if one can afford it is generally recognized, only a very small minority of people have felt it their duty to curtail their comforts and luxuries very seriously on that account, and still less the comforts and luxuries of those dependent on them. Yet there can hardly be any doubt that, even if we allow for any indirect evil effects which might accrue, in most cases money given to any even tolerably well managed charity will do much more good by relieving the suffering of those in distress than would be done by using the same money to increase the pleasure of a person who is at all tolerably comfortable by enabling him to have a more pleasant house, better furniture, more tobacco, more holiday travel, etc.[4]

Much the same might be said of entire nations. The contrast between Sweden or the U.S., on the one hand, and Haiti or Chad or Bolivia, on the other, is as stark as that between a businessman and a starving beggar. And what holds for efficient private charities holds for efficient foreign aid. The dollars spent on aid would do more good than if left in the taxpayers' pockets. For the distress to be relieved is often extreme. Yet few citizens have felt it their duty to curtail their comforts and luxuries very seriously on that account. And accordingly no country has notably lowered its own high standard of living in an attempt to achieve greater equality among nations. Once again, in the case of countries as in that of individuals, the hungry man gets a sliver, the fat man gets the rest of the pie.

If, then, the implications of the principle of parity appear so radically at variance with common practice, what are we to say? That the conduct of persons and nations does indeed fall far short of their obligations? That the principle's implications are not as radical as they appear? That the principle is mistaken, its concern for others excessive? Ewing favors this third alternative and opts for a "common-sense morality":

> Ordinarily we consider that we are much more under an obligation to some people than to others. We admit indeed that we are under some obligation to help anyone in need, but we feel a very much stronger obligation to promote the happiness of our own family, as is shown by the general attitude to appeals for charity. It is clear that the money spent by a man in order to provide his son with a university education could save the lives of many people who were perishing of hunger in a famine, yet most people would rather blame than praise a man who should deprive his son of a university education on this account.[5]

Whether for ourselves, our family, our friends, or our country, many would agree that "charity begins at home."

It may be wondered, however, whether those on short rations would readily agree with these verdicts of "common sense," and whether we would see things quite the same way were we in their places. Yet moral principles, remember, should work both ways; they should be universalizable. For preferential treatment to be justified, for ourselves or for the privileged generally, there should be a difference that makes a difference, morally. But what is so special about us? Are we perhaps more deserving than others? Have we merited our good fortune and they their misfortune? Do whole peoples, or the less-advantaged segments of society, deserve their disadvantages?

This clash of viewpoints recalls the one in chapter 5's Background Remarks and the methods suggested for resolving it. Parity's requirements may be startling, and at variance with majority practice, it is true; but that is no argument against it. The morally pertinent question is whether the rule conflicts with the considered moral judgments of the majority, or rather with mere unreflective assumptions and rationalizing self-interest.

The chapter's arguments can help to focus this issue, and in turn be focused by it. In each case — pets, whistle-blowing, graft, freer trade, immigration, leaving the group, guaranteed income, foreign aid — try to estimate realistically what equal concern for the good of all persons or peoples would dictate. Then, if the verdict looks unappealing, consider whether it is morally or just humanly repugnant. The ethical is not synonymous with the easy.

FURTHER READING

Joel Feinberg, ed., *Reason and Responsibility* (Belmont, Calif., 1965), part 6 ("Self-Love and the Claims of Morality").

William Frankena, *Ethics*, 2d ed. (Englewood Cliffs, 1973), pp. 45–55.

Victor Grassian, *Moral Reasoning: Ethical Theory and Some Contemporary Moral Problems* (Englewood Cliffs, 1981), pp. 144–51 ("Ethical Egoism").

Garth Hallett, *Christian Moral Reasoning: An Analytic Guide* (Notre Dame, 1983), chapter 5, section G ("The Order of Charity"); chapter 8, sections A ("My Good versus Others'") and C ("Fraternity versus Equality").

E. D. Klemke, A. David Kline, Robert Hollinger, eds., *Philosophy: The Basic Issues* (New York, 1982), part 11 ("Economic and Social Injustice").

Paul Ramsey, *Basic Christian Ethics* (New York, 1950), chapter 5, section ii ("Non-Preferential Love and Duties to Oneself").

Gerald Runkle, *Ethics: An Examination of Contemporary Moral Problems* (New York, 1982), pp. 306–22 ("Distributive Justice").

Peter Singer, *Practical Ethics* (Cambridge, 1979), chapter 8 ("Rich and Poor")

SAMPLE ANALYSIS-EVALUATION: #5 (IMMIGRATION)

1. *Streamlined Version:*

   (1) The interests of those presently in the United States should be given precedence over the interests of would-be immigrants. (This wording results from applying the Principle of Charity to: "Our immigration policy has to be designed in the interests of the United States." A purely egoistic interpretation, looking solely to the interests of present residents, would be too plainly false; an egalitarian interpretation, putting the interests of immigrants on a par with those of residents, would disconnect the premise from the conclusion.)

   (C) The American tradition of hospitality to immigrants should be curtailed or abandoned.

2. *Diagram:*

   ```
   (1)
    |
   (C)
   ```

3. *Evaluation of the Premise:*

   "No one," writes John Rawls, "deserves his place in the distribution of native endowments, any more than one deserves one's initial starting place in society." And what holds for individuals holds for groups, classes, and entire peoples. Americans have no special claim to their favored position. Thus self-preference is no more justified collectively than it is individually.

4. *Evaluation of the Connection:*

   Whether the premise entails the conclusion depends on these three considerations: (1) How strongly, according to the premise, should the interests of those presently in the U.S. be preferred to those of would-be immigrants?

Sample Analysis-Evaluation: #5 (Immigration) 147

Should equal benefit for a resident be preferred at a ratio of two-to-one, five-to-one, ten-to-one? (2) How much, if at all, would those now in the U.S. benefit from curbing immigration? (3) How notably, on the other hand, would immigrants benefit from being allowed to enter? The first question seems irresolvable through further application of the Principle of Charity. The second is rendered murky by the indefiniteness of the proposed reductions in immigration. Supposedly the benefits would be proportionate to the reductions. The fewer immigrants were admitted, the fewer would use up welfare funds, compete for present jobs, consume the nation's resources, pollute the environment, occupy available space, and so forth. However, more people mean more jobs as well as more competition for them. And the U.S. has more space and resources than most countries. Thus, looking back on what immigrants have contributed in the past and forward to the resentments that might result from too sharp a division between haves and have-nots in the world, and reflecting on the priority of human values over material, one may wonder whether a restrictive policy would be in the best interests of Americans themselves. (Figuratively speaking, it may be doubted whether dismantling the Statue of Liberty and using the materials for more "practical" purposes would benefit the people of this country.) The benefits to immigrants, on the other hand, are clear. They come seeking relatives, economic betterment, political asylum. Thus the argument's connection, too, looks weak.

CHAPTER 8

Morality and Law

"If it's wrong, there should be a law against it." "If there is a law against it, it shouldn't be done." Though simplistic, these familiar thoughts contain much truth. But how much? Law is such an important, pervasive aspect of our lives, from birth through schooling, marriage, and employment to the grave, that it merits special notice in a survey of morality. The arguments and background essays of this chapter, therefore, focus first on the question of legislating morality, second on the question of obedience to law.

A. LEGISLATION

ARGUMENTS FOR ANALYSIS AND EVALUATION

1. LEGALIZING HARD DRUGS

"Jack, I've been forced to change my mind about drugs. Let anybody put anything he wants into his mouth or his veins. Make hard drugs as legal as alcohol. Let everybody take charge of his own bad habits, and I really think we'll all be better off. If addicts didn't have to steal, society would no longer have to spend impossible sums trying to protect people from addicts. As for protecting addicts from themselves, from destroying themselves, I no longer think that's society's job. What finally persuaded me was the record here in New York State. Two years ago Governor Rockefeller put through the toughest drug law in the country. Selling just one ounce of the hard stuff means a mandatory prison term of at least 15 years. It can mean prison for life. Yet, even

this brutish escalation of punishment to barbarous levels has had no effect whatever, neither on drug addiction nor on drug-related crime. I conclude you cannot protect people from themselves. Therefore, I would remove the penalties from all victimless crimes, not only drugs. Also gambling, drunkenness, prostitution, homosexuality, and so on. If these activities lead to violent crime, prosecute the thief, the mugger, the rapist, but put public safety ahead of public morals. You'll charge me with endangering the safety of children, but kids learn by example, Jack. Make each person free to take pot, to take cocaine, to take rat poison, and you begin to make him responsible for his own acts. That's got to be better, Jack, for us and for our kids."
      Shana Alexander, dialoging with James J. Kilpatrick on *60 Minutes*, September 11, 1975.

2. SEAT BELTS

"Legislation to make Michigan the first state to require motorists to wear seat belts won unanimous praise at its debut Thursday.

 "'Seat belts are the most effective device ever developed for saving lives and preventing injuries,' Chrysler Corp. Chairman Lee Iacocca said at a hearing held by the House Insurance Committee. 'They work better than any safety device ever invented. The only problem is that we have to use them,' he said, noting that only about nine percent of motorists wear them.

"The Michigan proposal, sponsored by Rep. David Hollister, D-Lansing, would require drivers and passengers riding in the front seat of most motor vehicles to buckle up during travel.

"'The primary reason people are opposed to such a law is ideological,' Iacocca said. 'They believe such a law is an intrusion on their freedom, and they are willing to let hundreds die and thousands be injured in the name of that ideology.'"
      "Seat-Belt Bill Wins Praise at House Hearing," *Detroit Free Press*, May 21, 1982, p. A-3.

3. ABORTION

"The link between the innocence of abortion and a permissive abortion policy is a liberal social theory. Such a theory divides the acts performed by responsible human agents into two categories: those that cause harm to others (public acts) and those that do not (private acts). It is permissible for the state to use coercion against the performance of (at least some) public acts, by passing laws backed by sanctions prohibiting such acts. But it is absolutely impermissible for it to employ coercion against private acts. Any law regulating private activities is an illegitimate intrusion into the realm of personal liberty. Although abortion ostensibly displays this dimension of interpersonal injury, since causing a person's death is normally counted as causing injury, in fact the fetus does not possess the capacity to be injured. Abortion therefore belongs in the private realm, along with other medical procedures undertaken with the informed consent of the patient. Restrictive or moderate abortion laws protect no one against the use of force or fraud; therefore, they lack moral justification."

L. W. Sumner, *Abortion and Moral Theory* (Princeton, 1981), p. 16 (not his view).

4. PROSTITUTION

"After an examination of both positions, the arguments in favor of decriminalization seem to emerge with compelling force. Yes, prostitutes are unfairly treated under the law in terms of their being given virtually automatic criminal status. Yes, society's out-of-sight, out-of-mind attitude, which makes brothels, massage parlors and the call-girl business less objectionable to the public than streetwalkers, is hypocritical. Yes, statutes against soliciting may, as the A.C.L.U. contends, be violations of the right to freedom of speech as guaranteed under the First Amendment. Yes, law-enforcement resources, being limited, might be better used against graver types of crime. Yes, efforts to control prostitution, whether through strict measures aimed at suppressing it entirely or through tolerating it in the form of legalized outlets, have historically met with scant success anywhere."

George M. Anderson, "Prostitution: Old Problem, New Conflicts," *America*, April 16, 1977, pp. 353–54.

5. EUTHANASIA

"Does this mean, in the last analysis, that in a conflict between the two values (relief of suffering and the prolongation of life) the law finally comes down on the side of sustaining life? As a whole, yes, although short of ending life, the law certainly supports the physician in every effort to relieve suffering.

"Although this view may seem harsh, the alternative is even more undesirable. For if physicians were authorized by law to decide when the quality of a patient's life warranted its discontinuance, and if the law authorized the physician to act to end life or to omit treatment which would sustain life, then the result would be, obviously, a complete breakdown in the trust relationship between patient and physician. Good medical care cannot proceed effectively without that trust. If the patient had not only the burden of dealing with suffering but also of wondering when and how the physician might choose to end his or her life, the basis for medical care would be entirely changed. The law is right to resist giving such authority to doctors in life-or-death decisions."

> Thomas C. Oden, "A Cautious View of Treatment Termination," *Christian Century*, January 21, 1976, p. 41.

6. NUDISM

"Surely one freedom of those in the majority is to have the kind of social and aesthetic environment that they desire in the moral mode. It is with this in mind that nudists are asked to disrobe only in private or in camps segregated for that purpose. If the clash between the majority and minority over nudism meant that nudists could appear anywhere in public, then in this case majority rights would be nugatory while the minority rights would be guaranteed."

> Raymond D. Gastil, "The Moral Right of the Majority to Restrict Obscenity and Pornography through Law," *Ethics* 86 (1975–1976): 232.

7. PORNOGRAPHY

"If one views pornography as a case of expression of ideas, its commercial form would have to be curbed on the basis of Mill's harm principle. The harm it produces are (1) lowering the tone of the life of commerce and the areas in which it takes place, (2) providing offense to the general population who cannot possibly avoid its advertising and marquees, (3) corrupting the morality of those on whom it is foisted, and (4) causing antisocial and violent actions against society. These are substantial and vastly outweigh the loss of freedom."

Gerald Runkle, *Ethics: An Examination of Contemporary Moral Problems* (New York, 1982), p. 381 (illustrative argumentation).

8. MARIHUANA

"On August 2, 1977, President Carter sent to the Congress a message on drug abuse. On the subject of marihuana he stated:

"'Marihuana continues to be an emotional and controversial issue. After four decades, efforts to discourage its use with stringent laws have still not been successful. More than 45 million Americans have tried marihuana and an estimated 11 million are regular users.

"'Penalties against possession of a drug should not be more damaging to an individual than the use of the drug itself; and where they are, they should be changed. Nowhere is this more clear than in the laws against the possession of marihuana in private for personal use. We can, and should, continue to discourage the use of marihuana, but this can be done without defining the smoker as a criminal. States which have already removed criminal penalties for marihuana use, like Oregon and California, have not noted any significant increase in marihuana smoking. The National Commission on Marihuana and Drug Abuse concluded 5 years ago that marihuana use should be decriminalized, and I believe it is time to implement those basic recommendations.'"

Congressional Digest, February 1979, p. 38.

BACKGROUND REMARKS

It is sometimes said that morality cannot be legislated. Yet only certain types of restraint—on pornography, say, or prostitution—elicit that remark. Similar complaints are seldom voiced against the prohibition of such immoral actions as murder, theft, assault, rape, libel, bribery, fraud, breach of contract. The pertinent question, therefore, is not so much *whether* morality should be legislated as *when*, *when not*, and *why*.

Mill's Rule

In *On Liberty* (1859) John Stuart Mill drew the following line between legitimate and illegitimate legislation:

> The object of this Essay is to assert one very simple principle. . . . That principle is, that the sole end for which mankind are warranted, individually or collectively, in interfering with the liberty of action of any of their number, is self-protection. That the only purpose for which power can be rightfully exercised over any member of a civilized community, against his will, is to prevent harm to others. His own good, either physical or moral, is not a sufficient warrant. He cannot rightfully be compelled to do or forbear because it will be better for him to do so, because it will make him happier, because in the opinions of others, to do so would be wise, or even right. These are good reasons for remonstrating with him, or reasoning with him, or persuading him, or entreating him, but not for compelling him, or visiting him with any evil in case he do otherwise. To justify that, the conduct from which it is desired to deter him must be calculated to produce evil to some one else. The only part of the conduct of any one, for which he is amenable to society, is that which concerns others. In the part which merely concerns himself his independence is, of right, absolute.[1]

This rule—"Hands off unless others are harmed!"—has proved extremely influential and is frequently cited today. It appears, for instance, in chapter 1 (exercise 1, #1d) and chapter 3 (exercise 2, j) and now in several of this section's arguments. It is the "ideological" reason Lee Iacocca mentions as a source of opposition to seat-belt laws (argument 2). It is the principle explicitly cited in argument 7 and spelled out in argument 3 on abortion. It is the position Shana Alexander adopts in argument 1, concerning not only drugs but "also gambling, drunkenness, prostitution, homosexuality, and so on." And it is relevant to the remaining four arguments as well.

Mill's Grounds

Only Alexander offers reasons for accepting Mill's position, and only one of her reasons coincides with his. It is better for all, she asserts, if each person is made responsible for his own acts. On this Mill agreed. "Mankind are greater gainers," he maintained, "by suffering each other to live as seems good to themselves, than by compelling each other to live as seems good to the rest."

One explanation might be that those who decide for themselves develop their own powers and grow as human beings. And Mill did in fact make much of this point. "The human faculties of perception, judgment, discriminative feeling, mental activity, and even moral preference, are exercised only in making a choice." If custom or law decides, then a person "gains no practice either in discerning or in desiring what is best." However, this objection would apply with equal force to any type of legislation. Laws against theft or embezzlement curb the ingenuity of criminals, laws against rape or assault narrow people's powers of decision, and so forth. So some other ground seems necessary to establish Mill's distinction between licit and illicit areas of restraint.

"The strongest of all the arguments," he wrote, "against the interference of the public with purely personal conduct is that, when it does interfere, the odds are that it interferes wrongly, and in the wrong place." In support of this contention he argued persuasively:

> With respect to his own feelings and circumstances, the most ordinary man or woman has means of knowl-

edge immeasurably surpassing those that can be possessed by anyone else. The interference of society to overrule his judgment and purposes in what only regards himself must be grounded on general presumptions; which may be altogether wrong, and even if right, are as likely as not to be misapplied to individual cases, by persons no better acquainted with the circumstances of such cases than those are who look at them merely from without. In this department, therefore, of human affairs, Individuality has its proper field of action.

The problem with this reasoning, once again, is that it seems to cut both ways. All laws, and not just those Mill would ban, affect individuals in ways they know best. In every department of human affairs—murder or pornography, marriage or adultery, tax fraud or abortion—each person is most conversant with his or her own feelings and circumstances. People tempted to embezzle, pilfer, or fudge on their tax returns are more intimately acquainted with their particular problems, needs, and desires than are those who make the laws. The Youngstown workers prevented by property laws from taking over a doomed plant knew far better than the makers of the laws just how the plant's closing would affect them, their families, and their town. In *every* instance legislators take a larger view than that of individuals and go by "general presumptions"; they have to if they are to serve the common good. So Mill's argument appears to prove too much. It tells against all legislation and not just the kind he opposed.

Alternative Guidelines

A thinker of Mill's stature cannot be dismissed on the strength of a single objection to a single argument, even the most plausible of those he advanced and the one he most stressed. Replies might be suggested, further grounds be urged for his position. It might be found, for example, that the verdicts of Mill's single rule largely coincide with those of the less problematic guidelines proposed by Basil Mitchell.[2] To discriminate good legislation from bad, he offers the following norms (the parenthetical remarks are mine):

(1) So far as possible, privacy should be respected. (Hence, perhaps, the absence of laws against masturbation.)
(2) It is, as a rule, bad to pass laws which are difficult to enforce and whose enforcement tends, therefore, to be patchy and inequitable. (Think, for instance, of a law against smoking marihuana.)
(3) It is bad to pass laws which do not command the respect of most reasonable people who are subject to them. (Consider, for example, the weak public backing for Prohibition.)
(4) One should not pass laws which are likely to fail in their object (e.g., laws against suicide) or produce a great deal of suffering, or other evils such as blackmail (or, e.g., windfalls for organized crime, when drugs or gambling are made illegal; or a rise in unorganized crime due to the drugs' high cost).
(5) Legislation should be avoided which involves punishing people (e.g., drug addicts, alcoholics) for what they very largely cannot help.

These five points are apparently proposed as helpful rules of thumb, not as airtight norms admitting no exceptions. Each consideration should be kept in view and may often prove decisive, but not always. Thus in (1) Mitchell says "so far as possible" and in (2) "as a rule," and though he adds no such proviso in (4), it is clear that the "other evils" may not be serious enough to outweigh the benefits of legislation. Drug prohibition has serious drawbacks, but so does legalization. The prohibition of abortion results in clandestine operations and so endangers women's lives; yet legalization encourages abortion and threatens fetal life. Again, a declaration of war, as after Pearl Harbor, and the drafting of men for military service are bound to "produce a great deal of suffering" but are not therefore ruled out. The victory of Hitler, Mussolini, and Tojo might have occasioned still more suffering.

If Mitchell's five criteria, realistically applied, excluded all or most of the laws that Mill's rule disallows, then his principle might serve at least as a safe statistical guide. It would hold in the majority of cases. However, when it applied, when not, and why, we would not know save by referring back to the rules from which it derived. They alone would give us inner understanding of where to draw the line. And that, remember, was the question we set out to clarify: When and why may morality be legislated, when not?

So those five rules are the ones we can apply, as a start, to any debated legislation, including that in the arguments of this chapter. It is not enough that a law achieve some worthwhile purpose, say the protection of lives. Does it also pass these five tests? Does any of the criteria tell against it decisively? Or is there perhaps some other objection to it, not covered by Mitchell's list? The present brief introduction has not touched all bases, as the student will soon discover who reads on in the suggested readings.

FURTHER READING

William P. Alston and Richard B. Brandt, eds., *The Problems of Philosophy*, 3d ed. (Boston, 1978), part III, B ("The Authority of Governments and Individual Liberty").

Tom L. Beauchamp, ed., *Ethics and Public Policy* (Englewood Cliffs, 1975), chapter 5 ("Moral Enforcement").

Peter A. French, ed., *Philosophical Explorations* (Morristown, N.J., 1975), part II ("Government, Law, and the Public Morals").

Victor Grassian, *Moral Reasoning: Ethical Theory and Some Contemporary Moral Problems* (Englewood Cliffs, 1981), pp. 217–30 ("Liberty and the Enforcement of Morality").

Burton M. Leiser, *Liberty, Justice, and Morals: Contemporary Value Conflicts*, 2d ed. (New York, 1979), pp. 1–30.

Gerald Runkle, *Ethics: An Examination of Contemporary Moral Problems* (New York, 1982), pp. 386–412 ("Freedom of Action").

SAMPLE EVALUATION, of a Law from Argument 1 (Legalizing Hard Drugs), Using Mitchell's Critieria:

The Law: Prohibition of the Use and Sale of (e.g.) Heroin in the U.S.

(1) With present safeguards (e.g., the requirement of a search warrant to enter someone's home) the law occasions no special problems with regard to privacy.

(2) Experience has shown how difficult it is to curb either the sale or the use of heroin. And the difficulty seems predictable. The heroin trade is so lucrative and demand is so easily met (ten square miles of poppies suffice to supply the whole American market) that as soon as one source is cut off (e.g., Turkey) another opens up (e.g., Colombia or the Golden Triangle). If enforcement is strengthened in one area (e.g., Florida), the drug flow shifts elsewhere (e.g., Louisiana or Tennessee). If one pusher is jailed, others eagerly take the place he leaves vacant (like backup players waiting on the bench). As for curbing use (the law's chief motive), prohibition probably does at least as much to spread addiction as to limit it. For by pushing up the

price it creates a cadre of supermotivated salesmen, eager to make addicts of nonaddicts, whatever their age. Addicts finance their addiction largely by peddling drugs.

(3) Laws against hard drugs like heroin presently enjoy stronger backing in the U.S. than did the prohibition of alcoholic beverages. Despite the largely negative judgments of experts on existing legislation, little popular debate on the subject has occurred. Attention has focused on "soft" drugs like hashish and marihuana.

(4) Besides failing in their object (see #2), the present restrictions entail notable evils. They bring huge profits to organized crime and spread unorganized crime (a major source of funds to finance the habit). They corrupt police forces, locally and nationally, more than any other current type of legislation. They exact large expenditures for enforcement and imprisonment, and crowd already overcrowded courts and prison facilities. And they wreck addicts' lives in a way that British laws, for example, do not. Whereas in the British system addicts register to purchase drugs and so can be identified and assisted, in the American system they remain unknown criminals and so are less readily reached. Whereas in the British system addicts need deal only with their addiction, and do so fairly successfully with the help of remedial programs, in the American system addiction tends to become an obsessive problem, blotting out all else, because it is so expensive. Unless he makes a move on his own to reach out for help, an addict is likely to be socially, psychologically, financially, humanly ruined by his habit.

(5) Addicts largely cannot help taking the dose they crave in order to relieve the distress they increasingly feel without it.

Overall, therefore, in the light of 2, 4, and 5 the law seems a bad one.

B. OBEDIENCE

ARGUMENTS FOR ANALYSIS AND EVALUATION

1. CHARITY VERSUS THE LAW

"Legalism is 'formal' obedience, 'material' avoidance.... It shuts its eyes to the fact that in some situations what is legally right is morally wrong, when the total context and consequences are weighed. Last March an Episcopal minister in New York hacksawed off the utility company's locks on gas and electric meters in a tenement of poor people, to prevent accident, illness, and exposure. Here was a clear case of contralegalism. He broke the letter of the laws on trespass and burglary to prevent the unjust victimization of tenants whose landlords were scofflaws in arrears on Consolidated Edison's bills."

Joseph Fletcher, *Moral Responsibility: Situation Ethics at Work* (Philadelphia, 1967), p. 165.

2. CAR THEFT

"Even the thieves are able to justify their work. A veteran, very professional thief who lives in New Jersey reasons, 'What I do is good for everybody. First of all, I create work. I hire men to deliver the cars, work on the numbers, paint them, give them paper, maybe drive them out of state, find customers. That's good for the economy. Then I'm helping working people to get what they could never afford otherwise. A fellow wants a Cadillac but he can't afford it. So I get this fellow a nice car at a price he can afford; maybe I save him as much as $2,000. Now he's happy. But so is the guy who lost his car. He gets a nice new Cadillac from the insurance company—without the dents and scratches we had to take out. The Cadillac company—they're happy too because they sell another Cadillac.

"'The only people who don't do so good is the insurance company. But they're so big that nobody cares *personally*. They got a budget for this sort of thing anyway. So here I am, a guy without an education, sending both my kids to college, giving my family a good home, making other people happy. Come on now—who am I really hurting?'"

Peter Hellman, "Stealing Cars Is a Growth Industry,"
New York Times Magazine, June 20, 1971, p. 45.

3. PAYING TAXES

"Are tax laws, then, merely penal laws [not obliging in conscience]? This opinion seems solidly probable, at least regarding some of the newer forms of taxation. Taxes have become too numerous and complicated for the ordinary citizen to handle, are accompanied by disproportionate penalties, and are often deducted at the source so that the citizen is not even trusted to do his duty; the state shows that it simply wants its money and makes no appeal to the public conscience. These are the usual indications of a purely penal law. It is therefore difficult to see a moral fault in a man who in general meets his tax obligation and supports the state, but occasionally evades a tax here and there, provided that in doing so he does not resort to such practices as lying or bribery."

Austin Fagothey, *Right and Reason*,
1st ed. (St. Louis, 1953), p. 477.

4. ABORTION

"Consider . . . the case of the doctor who has to decide whether he is justified in performing an illegal abortion. If he only has a prima facie duty to obey the law it looks as though he might justifiably decide that in this case his prima facie obligation is overridden by more stringent conflicting obligations. Or, if he is simply a utilitarian, it appears that he might rightly conclude that the consequences of disobeying the abortion law would be on the whole and in the long run less deleterious than those of obeying. But this is simply a mistake. The doctor would inevitably be neglecting the most crucial factor of all, namely, that in performing the abortion he was disobeying the law. And imagine what would happen if everyone went around disobeying the law. The alternatives are obeying the law and general disobedience. The choice is between any social order and chaos.

"Such an argument, while perhaps overdrawn, is by no means uncommon."
>Richard A. Wasserstrom, "The Obligation to Obey the Law," in H. Bedau, ed., *Civil Disobedience: Theory and Practice* (Indianapolis, 1969), pp. 256–57.

5. ILLEGAL DEMONSTRATIONS

"The city government obtained a court injunction directing us to cease our activities until our right to demonstrate had been argued in court. The time had now come for us to counter their legal maneuver with a strategy of our own. Two days later, we did an audacious thing. We disobeyed a court order.

"We did not take this radical step without prolonged and prayerful consideration. Planned, deliberate civil disobedience had been discussed as far back as the meeting at Harry Belafonte's apartment in March. There, in consultation with some of the closest friends of the movement, we had decided that if an injunction was issued to thwart our demonstrations, it would be our duty to violate it. To some, this will sound contradictory and morally indefensible. We, who contend for justice, and who oppose those who will not honor the law of the Supreme Court and the rulings of federal agencies, were saying that we would overtly violate a court order. Yet we felt that there were persuasive reasons for our position.

"When the Supreme Court decision on school desegregation was handed down, leading segregationists vowed to thwart it by invoking 'a century of litigation.' There was more significance to this threat than many Americans imagined. The injunction method has now become the leading instrument of the South to block the direct-action civil-rights drive and to prevent Negro citizens and their white allies from engaging in peaceable assembly, a right guaranteed by the First Amendment. You initiate a nonviolent demonstration. The power structure secures an injunction against you. It can conceivably take two or three years before any disposition of the case is made. The Alabama courts are notorious for 'sitting on' cases of this nature. This has been a maliciously effective, pseudo-legal way of breaking the back of legitimate moral protest.

"We had anticipated that this procedure would be used in

Birmingham. It had been invoked in Montgomery to outlaw our car pool during the bus boycott. It had destroyed the protest movement in Talladega, Alabama. It had torpedoed our effort in Albany, Georgia. It had routed the N.A.A.C.P. from the state of Alabama. We decided, therefore, knowing well what the consequences would be and prepared to accept them, that we had no choice but to violate such an injunction."

Martin Luther King, Jr., *Why We Can't Wait* (New York, 1963), pp. 68–69.

6. STUDENT SIT-INS

"In the heyday of student riots (ca. 1968–70), a common pattern of conduct was for a group of students to stage a sit-in in the dean's office or to occupy the administration building, protesting whatever they were protesting, and insisting that they were going to stay there until their demands, which were not negotiable, were met; and sometimes they had firearms, which they at least threatened to use if attempts were made to force them out. Almost always they made a shambles of the offices which they occupied, and one way or another they broke quite a number of laws, sometimes federal, certainly state, as well as plenty of college/university regulations. They claimed that they were undertaking the sit-ins on principle, protesting the war, or their institution's participation in war-related research, or its supporting an ROTC division, etc. In the end they agreed to come out, but they often—and this is the relevance of the story—demanded as a condition of agreeing to come out that they be given amnesty for any lawbreaking which they had committed. . . .

"I criticize the authorities for giving in to the students' demands that they should not be made to pay for their principles. They should have insisted that people who claim to believe in a principle sufficiently to be a martyr, that is, a witness, for it should be prepared to wear the martyr's crown. And I criticize the students similarly: they demeaned themselves and their professions by demanding amnesty and by making acceptance of that demand a necessary condition of their agreeing to come out. I criticize them for professing principles and yet not knowing what it is to have a principle, namely, to be prepared to suffer for it."

A. D. Woozley, "Civil Disobedience and Punishment," *Ethics* 86 (1975–1976): 327–28.

7. PROTESTING INJUSTICE

"I would say that there are very few unjust laws in most of our northern communities. There are some unjust laws, I think, on the housing question and some others, but on the whole the laws are just. But there is injustice, and there are communities which do not work with vigor and with determination to remove that injustice. In such instances I think men of conscience and men of good will have no alternative but to engage in some kind of civil disobedience in order to call attention to the injustices, so that the society will seek to rid itself of that overall injustice."
Martin Luther King, Jr., quoted in Hugo A. Bedau, ed., *Civil Disobedience: Theory and Practice* (New York, 1969), p. 112.

8. SYMBOLIC DISOBEDIENCE

"When the two Berrigan brothers and their six companions entered the G.E. plant outside of Philadelphia on Sept 9 and poured blood on the blueprints of the nuclear Mark 12 weapons, they were trying to get us to see what I try to get my students to see—the threat to our very survival constituted by nuclear weapons.

"But why violate the law? Why destroy government property? Why don't they teach about it as I do? Answer: they believe they are teaching by their actions. They expect to land in jail for their actions. They hope to rouse us from our lethargy by their suffering. They want to show us that we can do something about it, if we are willing to pay the price.

"'Well, why can't they just say that?' They have said it, over and over again, since 1964. Dan Berrigan has written about 33 books—almost all of them bearing on this point. He has lectured in over 100 colleges and universities on several continents on this topic. Philip Berrigan has written five books and lectured all over this country hundreds of times for 15 years.

"Despite all this, they see the danger growing worse, not less. . . .

"But couldn't they do it some other way than breaking the law? The law they broke is not God's law. Turn the case around and ask, 'Would it have been wrong for a German priest to go into the factory where Hitler's workers were making gas chambers and pour blood on the blueprints and damage the metal with hammers? . . . Everything that Hitler did was legal, once he became head of state. He made the law, but he made many evil laws. When our government shields the preparations for deaths, all our deaths, under the name of law, we desecrate law as Hitler did.

"We don't do it openly because we are still a free people. We hide from the people our preparations for their death. We make them pay for the nuclear cyanide that we will breathe in after the first nuclear exchange.

"The Berrigans and their friends want to break this process. They want us to choose life, instead of death. They show us dramatically that such a choice may cost much. They give us a good example of being ready to pay with their freedom to warn us of our danger."

Richard McSorley, in *National Jesuit News*,
November 1980.

BACKGROUND REMARKS

For Socrates the issue of obedience to law became a very personal matter when an Athenian jury found him guilty of atheism and corrupting the young and decreed that he should die by drinking hemlock. According to one of Plato's early dialogs, as Socrates awaited execution, a friend of his named Crito visited him in prison and urged him to escape. There was still time; it could easily be arranged. Think of your children, pleads Crito; think of us your friends and of our reputation, when people see we have not helped you as we might have.

In Socrates' ears the arguments of the state and its laws ring more persuasively. "What is it you intend to do?" he imagines them asking as he plans his escape. "By this action of yours do you not aim to destroy us, the laws, and indeed the whole city, as far as in you lies? Or do you think it possible for a city not to be destroyed if the verdicts of its courts have no force but are nullified and set at naught by private individuals?" Socrates might protest that the city has wronged him, that its sentence is unjust and therefore he may seek to evade it. But to this objection he imagines the laws replying: "Was that the agreement between us, Socrates?"

> We have given you birth, nurtured you, educated you, we have given you and all other citizens a share of all the good things we could. Even so, by giving every Athenian the opportunity, after he has reached manhood and observed the affairs of the city and us the laws, we proclaim that if we do not please him, he can take his possessions and go wherever he pleases. Not one of our laws raises any obstacle or forbids him, if he is not satisfied with us or the city, if one of you wants to go and live in a colony or wants to go anywhere else, and keep his property. We say, however, that whoever of you remains, when he sees how we conduct our trials and manage the city in other ways, has in fact come to an agreement with us to obey our instructions. We say that the one who disobeys does wrong . . . because, in spite of his agreement, he neither obeys us nor, if we do something wrong, does he try to persuade us to do better. Yet we only propose things, we do not issue savage commands to do whatever we order; we give two alternatives, either to persuade us or to do what we say.[3]

When the laws, speaking thus through Socrates' mouth, have finished their plausible plea, Crito has nothing to say in reply. "Very well, Crito," Socrates concludes, "let us so act, since so the God leads." He stays and drinks the poison.

Implicit in the answer of the laws is Socrates' solution to a recurring problem. The very existence of organized society requires that there be laws and that they be obeyed. Yet many laws are imperfect and some are very bad. So what are we to do? Pick the ones we approve and follow only those? In that case there would be no genuine obedience, but each person would do as he or she preferred and society would slip into chaos. Does it follow then that we should obey come what may, indiscriminately? That too sounds a hard saying, given the monstrous nature of some legislation, say in Hitler's Germany or in Stalin's Russia. So where does the just mean lie? What set of conditions may be stated for obeying and not obeying that will avoid excessive respect for law on the one hand and exaggerated freedom on the other?

The Socratic solution, briefly put, is this: In a free country, if you choose to stay and if you fail to persuade, then you should obey. This formula makes some provision for bad laws. If the whole system is bad, you can leave. If you disapprove of some particular order or enactment, you can work to get it changed (you can lobby, campaign, vote, plead your case, appeal to a higher court). But with these concessions made, the rule of law still stays basically intact. Whether good or bad, any law that remains a law should be obeyed.

Socrates, then, should accept the court's ruling in his regard. The minister in argument 1 should put away his hacksaw. The auto thief in argument 2 should stop his thieving. Taxpayers should ignore the reasoning in argument 3 and pay in full. The doctor in argument 4, the students in argument 6, activists like King in argument 5 and the Berrigans in argument 8 should desist from their illegal activities. A law is a law.

Yet are there no exceptions, we might ask (speaking up where Crito fell silent)? Are there no occasions when even a reasonable law may be disobeyed? Imagine a motorist, say, driving on a freeway. Suddenly a dog runs out; the driver swerves into another lane; her passenger utters an exclamation, clutches his chest, complains of pain, and shows other clear symptoms of a heart attack. So now she is doing 75 rather than 55 to get him to an emergency ward as quickly as she can. Is her speeding wrong? Surely not. Yet it breaks the law. So it would appear that more leeway is needed than Socrates' few conditions provide. It is not enough to say, "You can leave, or you can stay and try to change the law; otherwise you must obey." She doesn't want to leave, and she doesn't want to change the law, but she does nothing wrong if on this occasion she violates a traffic law or two.

Such, I imagine, is the verdict most people would give. But why? What makes the difference? Why is this deviation clearly legitimate, while much other disobedience is not? Examining this single clear case more carefully, we may perhaps detect criteria with which to test the legitimacy of disobedience in less obvious cases like those in arguments 1 to 8.

Three conditions which are fulfilled in this instance and which would have to be satisfied in others, it would seem, for disobedience to be justified are the following:

(1) *The advantages of disobedience clearly outweigh those of obedience.*
There was some risk to herself and others from her speeding but not as much risk as there would have been to her passenger had she observed the speed limit. And her single violation would not erode respect for the law.

(2) *There is no better way to achieve the advantages.*
Delaying to get an ambulance, say, would have eliminated the risk to herself and other motorists from her speeding but would have greatly increased the danger to her passenger.

(3) *The person disobeying is fully informed on both counts.*
That is, the person is in a position to know that conditions 1 and 2 are satisfied. Thus the motorist knew her passenger was having a heart attack, that delay would be dangerous, that there was no better way. The case was relatively simple and she had good common sense.

To recognize clearly that these conditions really do account for our approval, assume that any one of the three was not fulfilled. Imagine, for instance, that the speeding motorist had no heart-attack victim in her car and no comparable reason for doing 75 rather than 55. Or imagine the attack occurred at home and an ambulance could conveniently be gotten. Or suppose that she merely had a hunch her passenger might be having a heart attack. In each such supposition, negating one of the conditions, our verdict would alter. Justification would cease for her doing 75 or running red lights.

This set of three conditions is not a blank check for would-be-violators. It is not an open invitation to wholesale disregard for the law. The third condition, in particular — the requirement of full knowledge — is often not met. Thus a typical violator of the 55-mile-an-hour limit, for example, has not done research comparable to that of the authors of the law — on accidents, fatalities, gas consumption, energy needs, and the rest — and reached the conclusion that the law he or she is breaking is a bad one and need not be obeyed. Such disobedience reflects no serious study or deliberation. Accordingly it is not justified by our set of three conditions. The third criterion is not satisfied.

These new stipulations, then, look promising. But to see how reliable they are as general guides let us apply them, for instance, to Socrates' quite different situation. His decision concerned a judicial sentence, not a traffic law; and the sentence was unjust, whereas the traffic law supposedly is not. Yet despite these differences, the same triple test looks as appropriate as before and seems to yield an equally reasonable verdict.

The answer to the first question depends this time on Socrates' innocence. Were he guilty as charged and were the death sentence just, there would be no clear advantage in his evading the penalty for his crimes. The first condition would not be met. Given his innocence, however, there seems a clear advantage in his not being put to death.

The second condition, too, was verified, since there was no other way—no legal way—for him to save his life. He had to escape. Finally, he knew without study or research that both conditions were fulfilled. He knew that he was innocent, that he would die if he stayed, that the only alternative was to escape.

So if we admit an exception in the motorist's case, shouldn't we admit one in his? She may speed to the hospital. May not Socrates escape from prison? Is not that disobedience similarly justified? If so, the three conditions that apply to both these cases may prove suitable for assessing most of the arguments above. For most of them concern similar situations. The minister in argument 1, who had no complaint with the laws he violated, may be comparable to the motorist. King, who disagreed with the injunction forbidding him to march, may resemble Socrates. And though the attitude of the thief in argument 2, of Fagothey in argument 3, and of the doctor in argument 4 is less clear, still, whether they accept or oppose existing legislation, we may ask the same three questions to arrive at a verdict: Do the advantages of disobedience clearly outweigh the disadvantages? Is there no better way to achieve the desired advantages? Is the person well informed on both counts?

The final three arguments introduce a new twist. Take the Berrigans, for example, in argument 8. Like King, they disagreed with some policies and laws (arms legislation); but unlike King, they violated, not the laws they opposed, but other laws (of property and trespass) against which they had no complaint. Nonetheless, the same threefold critique still seems applicable. The heart-attack victim is now the whole world in the grip of nuclear escalation. The most effective way, they believe, to keep the attack from being fatal is the means they have chosen. And they supposedly have done their homework; they have studied the issues and have weighed the alternatives. So may not their method be moral?

If not, is it because one or the other condition is not in fact fulfilled? Or do the three conditions prove somehow inadequate as a general test of legitimacy? Do they need further refinement so as to strike a more exact balance between excessive permissiveness and excessive respect for the law?

FURTHER READING

A. K. Bierman and James A. Gould, *Philosophy for a New Generation* (New York, 1970), part IV ("Up Against the Law, Citizen").
James L. Christian, *Philosophy: An Introduction to the Art of Wondering*, 3d ed. (New York, 1981), part V, chapter 2 ("Laws/Conscience").
E.D. Klemke, A. David Kline, and Robert Hollinger, eds., *Philosophy: The Basic Issues* (New York, 1982), part 12 ("Liberty versus Authority").
Burton M. Leiser, *Liberty, Justice, and Morals: Contemporary Value Conflicts*, 2d ed. (New York, 1979), chapter 12 ("Civil Disobedience").
Gerald Runkle, *Ethics: An Examination of Contemporary Moral Problems* (New York, 1982), pp. 412–24 ("Civil Disobedience").
Paula R. Struhl and Karsten J. Struhl, *Philosophy Now: An Introductory Reader* (New York, 1972), chapter 14 ("Resistance, Confrontation, and Revolution").
Peter Y. Windt, *An Introduction to Philosophy: Ideas in Conflict* (St. Paul, 1982), chapter 8 ("The Obligation to Obey the Law").

SAMPLE EVALUATION, Applying the Three Conditions to Argument 8 (Symbolic Disobedience)

(1) Did the Advantages of Disobedience Clearly Outweigh Those of Obedience?

The answer to this question depends on the replies to two others: Is current U.S. nuclear policy seriously mistaken, and would such symbolic disobedience help to reverse it? To the first of these two questions I would reply in the affirmative, but about the second I have doubts, and my answer overall must therefore be negative: no, it is not clear that the advantages of disobedience outweighed those of obedience. Briefly, my reasons go as follows.

Contemporary humanity's most pressing concern is to avoid a nuclear holocaust. This requires gradual reduction and eventual elimination of nuclear arms. This in turn requires that the present arms race somehow be reversed. Reason and experience suggest that the only way is for one of the two chief rivals in the race to no longer insist on superiority, or even equality with the other, but be willing to retain at most a credible deterrent. If the many billions of dollars that might thus be saved are desperately needed for domestic programs and international assistance, the obligation to retrench looks doubly urgent. Add the danger posed by U.S. reliance on nuclear reaction to nonnuclear aggression in Europe, our refusal to renounce first-use of atomic weapons, and our readiness to retaliate in kind if subjected to nuclear attack (thereby wiping out further tens of millions and perhaps the entire human race), and even in bare outline current U.S. policy looks extremely menacing. The Berrigans and their friends had reason to be alarmed, and to wish to alter the country's present course.

But what might their raid achieve? It would hardly alert people to "the threat to our very survival constituted by nuclear weapons," as McSorley argues. Everyone knows the danger. But many have the notion that a credible deterrent is not sufficient deterrence (the mere ability to devastate Russia would not deter the Russians from aggression) or that the way to negotiate arms reductions is to deal from strength (as though the Russians would react to that any differently than Americans do). And bashing Mark 12 nose cones or pouring blood on blueprints does not demonstrate the weaknesses of such thinking. As for more subtle psychological effects, consider three classes of people who might be influenced by the G.E. raid: those who already agreed with the demonstrators would not be converted to their position; those who disagreed would be antagonized; and those who were unsure about nuclear policy but sure that laws should be obeyed might be alienated by such disobedience—as doubtless many were. I realize that reality is more complex than such schemes and that a striking, symbolic act might somehow act as a catalyst; I just wish to suggest why the benefits were unclear. Polarization looks as likely a result as heightened awareness or concern.

(2) Was There No Better Way to Achieve the Advantages?

Doubts like those just expressed do not exist for legal means like writing, lecturing, lobbying, organizing, and so forth; the link is clear between such means and the ends desired. As for McSorley's argument that despite all the Berrigans' legal activities the danger was increasing, not decreasing—well, it increased more markedly after the raid took place. The argument does not bear scrutiny.

(3) Were the Eight Activists Fully Informed on Both Counts?

Enough basic facts concerning U.S. nuclear policy were fairly evident. Though the possession of nuclear arms, or of any arms in present circumstances, may be morally problematic, it was clear that the country's existing deterrent (e.g., Polaris and Trident submarines) is more than adequate; that additional arms are enormously expensive and therefore humanly and economically ruinous; that insisting on parity or superiority is no way to end an arms race; that such a race, if not reversed, will probably lead to global devastation. However, neither the efficacy of disobedience nor its superiority to alternative, legal means was obvious to the demonstrators. Nor, to judge from their writings and declarations, were they interested in such pragmatic considerations. Like many crusaders since the first ones stormed eastward to Jerusalem, they were more given to prayer and action than to the careful analysis of issues and methods. One openly declared he was not concerned about "results" — nor therefore, it would appear, about conditions like the three I have stated for legitimate disobedience to law.

Retrospect

Your choice of arguments in part two has led you to consider quite varied practical and theoretical issues. Now you may want to know how everything fits together. How do the chapters relate to one another? What is the larger picture? Those with theoretical leanings might find it enlightening to order the chapters' questions hierarchically, the particular within the general and the general within the more general, like the squares within squares of chapter 1. And the resulting overall clarity when each framework was in place might give them special satisfaction: they would feel they knew their way about in moral questions. However, most people are not theoretically inclined. For them a more stimulating way to cover the same ground, and equally instructive, would be the following.

Rather than focusing on arguments and issues, as till now, focus on the arguers instead. Examine your analyses and evaluations to see what they reveal about the authors of the arguments. Often the reasoning proved defective in some way. Sometimes it was very bad. Now the question can be "Why?" What went wrong? Was the person simply ill-informed? Was his or her grasp of logic inadequate for the task? Did faulty moral theory vitiate the whole process? Or was the real culprit the heart and not the head? Was the reasoning mere rationalization, and the verdict a foregone conclusion? Was the person just producing pretexts for doing as he or she pleased?

Think, for example, of the car thief's argument in chapter 8. To hear him tell it, he was a noble Good Samaritan, a modern Robin Hood. Yet if you picked his argument for scrutiny, you soon noticed crucial omissions. There was no mention, for instance, of higher insurance rates, of inconvenience or worse to those whose cars were stolen, of the gap between insurance payments and the cost of new cars, of the possibility that he or his helpers might get caught and go to jail. Yet the thief knew these and other facts as well as you or I. So was his argument a mere smoke screen? Was profit his real interest, not morality? But in that case why did he bother to argue his case at all? And how account for his being ready with such a plausible-sounding defense if it wasn't one he had used before, perhaps to himself?

Once you have formed a fairly clear picture of any single arguer, you can consider how typical he or she appears. Do the other arguments you looked at give the same impression? Do their shortcomings reveal the same root cause or causes? If so, what conclusions can you perhaps draw concerning people generally, including yourself? Are moral reasoners typically weak or strong on theory, well or badly informed, confused or clear-thinking, sincere or insincere, in their search for a solution?

What benefit, therefore, you can ask in conclusion, may be hoped for from a course like this? Would people be helped most by the theory, or the specific issues, or the training in moral reasoning, or by confronting questions morally and not asking merely "What's in it for me?" How great might the benefit be, realistically? Would the car thief give up thieving if he took a course like this? Would he be less likely to choose such a career if he took the course beforehand?

According to Socrates, study leads to better understanding, and better understanding leads, inevitably, to better, more ethical living. A person might know what people say is right, and do the opposite. He might write one thing in an exam and do another. But if he really *knew* what is right and why, he would do it; if he really *knew* what is wrong and why, he would avoid it. The car thief, for example, if personally convinced that stealing cars is wrong, would not steal cars. The main difficulty, Socrates held, would be getting him to recognize that stealing cars is wrong. And what that would require would be better, clearer thinking. The obstacle to right conduct lies chiefly in the intellect, not in the will.

Now, was Socrates right about this, do you think? Do your analyses and evaluations bear him out? Through reflections like these, your review of part two can extend to the course as a whole.

APPENDIX A

Further Arguments and Issues

This appendix supplements the concrete moral issues of part two with others that may interest teachers and students. It also offers practice in self-reliance. Arguments in newspapers, magazines, books, debates, conversations, and TV shows do not come ready-classified and backed by pertinent theoretical discussion. Nor do these. Students will need to discern on their own which of the considerations in chapters 5 to 8 are relevant to a given argument, and how.

ARGUMENTS FOR ANALYSIS AND EVALUATION

1. PRISONS

"Prisons don't make sense. If their purpose is to rehabilitate, there is abundant evidence to prove that even the best prisons don't really rehabilitate. If their purpose is to deter, they don't deter. The depressingly high rate of recidivism, repeaters returning for a second or third stay in prison, is testimony of the failure of prisons to deter.

"About all that prisons may be said to do is punish: God knows they punish. But singling out fellow citizens for punishment so barbaric assumes an arrogance that is unworthy of men subscribing to religious ideals.

"Our prisons, even the best of them, are not only failures, they are of their nature inhuman. Watch a lion, a bear, even a monkey penned up in a zoo cage and try to deny a rising sense that this is very nearly against nature. Yet we confine men and women, made to the image and likeness of God, to cages that are even more confining than those of a zoo.

"Beyond confinement, with its desiccation of the primal urge toward freedom, we condemn men to a period, sometimes a lifetime, of meaninglessness. We yoke them to useless work, by that act telling them clearly that they are worthless in the eyes of society.

"Prisons are not only useless but grossly dehumanizing. Their very existence allows us to turn away from reality. Prisons are dust bins that permit us to sweep some of our basic problems out of sight and out of mind. We need never ask such sticky questions as, 'Is there something about our consumer oriented society with acquisition of consumer goods repeatedly trumpeted as a major life goal that encourages people to steal?' We need never ask, 'Why do an increasing number find drug-taking a desirable alternative, knowing as most of them do the price of addiction?' Our prison population is our horror closet, crammed indecently with ugly debris, that allows us to show a neat and tidy living room to visitors — and more important, to ourselves."

Michael Mack, "Let's Begin to Eliminate Prisons," *U.S. Catholic*, October 1972, p. 14.

2. ANIMALS' RIGHTS

"Singer and Regan approach the question of animals' rights by focusing on a condemnation of what Singer calls 'speciesism,' which is defined as 'a prejudice or attitude of bias toward the interests of members of one's own species and against those of members of other species' (S, p. 7). The main thesis advanced by them is that if we cannot morally justify discriminating against other human beings on grounds of race or sex (for example) then, for exactly the same sorts of reasons, we cannot morally justify discriminatory treatment of animals. Just as there are no morally relevant considerations which warrant exploiting other humans for our own ends, so there are none to warrant the exploitation of nonhumans. Just as there is no difference between human groups (such as those of different races, sexes, or intelligence levels) with respect to their capacity to suffer, so there is none between humans and animals — at least those animals with highly complex nervous systems like our own. From this standpoint humans are animals *tout court* and, as such, do not stand in any position of natural superiority. This is not, of course, to deny any significant difference between humans and animals, and neither Singer nor Regan commits himself to this absurdity. Rather, it is to deny any moral superiority on the part of *Homo sapiens*."

Michael Fox, "'Animal Liberation': A Critique," *Ethics* 88 (1977–1978): 107–8.

3. REVERSE DISCRIMINATION

"It is generally agreed that in the past, and probably also in the present, women candidates have been discriminated against by procedures which have been structured so that a woman is less likely to get a position than a man, all other things being equal. This has been especially true in the case of the most prestigious jobs. There is also, I believe, some general feeling that the situation ought to be corrected. What is more controversial is whether justice requires anything further as compensation. Correcting the situation means not discriminating either in favor of men or in favor of women, but compensating women by reverse discrimination would be favoring women. The objections to the latter are well known. Such compensatory favoring will not compensate fairly. Those deprived of jobs through discrimination will not have them restored, since the compensatory measures will apply mainly to the new crop of candidates who are currently looking for jobs but have not sought them in the past. Moreover, only the most 'marketable' candidates will actually get the jobs, and there is no reason to believe that a candidate's marketability bears much proportion to past injustices suffered.

"The mistake in being guided by such objections lies in identifying jobs as the good which compensatory measures aim to restore. What I wish to argue is that it is not, primarily, jobs which have unjustly been taken from women in the past and which, as a matter of justice, should now be restored to them. Rather, past discriminatory measures in hiring, especially for the more prestigious positions, have deprived women of the more personal goods of self-esteem, esteem by others, an enriched view of themselves, and maximal inclusion in the community. It is these goods which can and ought to be restored to women by compensatory discrimination."

Anne C. Minas, "How Reverse Discrimination Compensates Women," *Ethics* 88 (1977–1978): 74–75.

4. NUCLEAR FREEZE

"The fallacy is one that Mr. Reagan favored in his rhetoric during his campaign for the Presidency and has repeated since he assumed office. It is the claim that an intensified build-up of nuclear forces by the United States will prove to be the most effective incentive for the Soviet Union to begin serious negotiations about arms control. Such an argument flies in the face of all the evidence available concerning the psychology that dominates the arms race between the Soviet Union and the United States. For nearly 40 years, the driving force in this contest has been fear and suspicion. Any increase by one side has led to demands for an increase by the other. Moscow can no more be expected to yield to intimidation in negotiations over nuclear arms than Washington is likely to be. The whole point behind the call for a nuclear freeze is to dramatically interrupt this cycle of stimulus and response."

"National Security and Nuclear Superiority,"
America, April 17, 1982, p. 291.

5. POLICE AND FIREFIGHTER STRIKES

"No state permits strikes by employees whose job is to protect the public safety. Although police and firefighters' strikes have occurred, they are always illegal — and wrong. As Governor Calvin Coolidge said during the Boston police strike of 1919, 'There is no right to strike against the public safety by anybody, anywhere, anytime.' A strike by police places us back in the state of nature, and this condition is just as bad as Thomas Hobbes said it was. Boston almost immediately became a cauldron of violence and looting in 1919. In Montreal in 1969, people were afraid to go outside their homes, and thousands acquired weapons for self-protection. As experience during police strikes has shown, it is not simply the lower classes or the criminal element that performs lawless acts, but middle-class and 'respectable' people as well. The results of firefighters' strikes are almost as bad. Fires are untended, buildings burn down, and lives are lost. Arsonists (often strikers) have a field day."

Gerald Runkle, *Ethics: An Examination of Contemporary Moral Problems* (New York, 1982), p. 217 (presenting one side of the issue).

6. DEMOCRATIZING MANAGEMENT

"Lodge and Nader and a lot of other good people have proposed that we have public and employee representatives on the boards of directors of every major corporation in the United States. How long can we kid ourselves that there is a managerial prerogative of secrecy for a company which has as much influence over our lives as IBM or U.S. Steel or General Motors? If people in the United States could elect directors to the boards of the Fortune 500 industrial and financial corporations, it would be more significant than most of the votes cast for members of state legislatures because these corporations are more significant for your life. Why do we say that the introduction of new technology, the location of plants, policies toward women, policies toward minorities, are private matters? Why is it in the United States today that we give corporations that leave New York City a federal subsidy by investment tax credit for leaving? What we need is to democratize and transform the corporation itself."

>Michael Harrington, "Corporate Collectivism: A System of Social Injustice," in *Ethics for Modern Life*, 2d ed., ed. Raziel Abelson and Marie-Louise Friquegnon (New York, 1982), pp. 467–68.

7. EDUCATION

"That the whole or any large part of the education of the people should be in State hands, I go as far as any one in deprecating. All that has been said of the importance of individuality of character, and diversity in opinions and modes of conduct, involves, as of the same unspeakable importance, diversity of education. A general State education is a mere contrivance for moulding people to be exactly like one another: and as the mould in which it casts them is that which pleases the predominant power in the government, whether this be a monarch, a priesthood, an aristocracy, or the majority of the existing generation; in proportion as it is efficient and successful, it establishes a despotism over the mind, leading by natural tendency to one over the body. An education established and controlled by the State should only exist, if it exist at all, as one among many competing experiments, carried on for the purpose of example and stimulus, to keep the others up to a certain standard of excellence."

>John Stuart Mill, *On Liberty*, chapter 5.

8. CAPITAL PUNISHMENT

"Donald R. Burrill argues that capital punishment actually violates a fundamental moral principle of our society. The conviction that every crime deserves an appropriate retribution must entail the power to 'undo' the penalty if the person judged guilty and duly punished is later found to be innocent. Once inflicted, the death penalty obviously cannot be undone. Furthermore, in violent crime there is frequently considerable ambiguity as to the responsibility of the assailant, and determination of his culpability before the law may not be easy. In these circumstances, how can such an absolute penalty as death be pronounced? The seriousness of the death sentence leads more often than not to an extended judicial appeal process which lasts for years and usually does not lead to execution (in 1964 out of 2620 persons convicted of murder, 81 were sentenced to death and only 2 were executed). This uncertainty and delay in punishment, say the penologists, negates any force of deterrence that the death penalty might possess."

Paul T. Jersild and Dale A. Johnson, eds.,
Moral Issues and Christian Response, 2d ed.
(New York, 1976), pp. 298–99.

9. HOMOSEXUALITY

"Some, much, even most homosexual activity may be morally exceptionable: so too is a good deal of heterosexual activity. In neither case is this necessarily so. Nor does it appear that homosexual relationships in themselves are necessarily more objectionable than heterosexual ones. I can see no good reason to doubt that it is possible for a homosexual to conduct his sexual life with prudence, beneficence, fairness and responsibility. If he does, there is no ground for moral complaint."

Ronald Atkinson, "The Morality of Homosexual
Behavior," in *Today's Moral Problems*, 2d ed.,
ed. Richard A. Wasserstrom (New York, 1979), p. 312.

10. PARENTS AND CHILDREN

"Suppose sisters Cecile and Dana are equally loved by their parents, even though Cecile was an easy child to care for, seldom ill, while Dana was often sick and caused some trouble as a juvenile delinquent. As adults, Dana is a struggling artist living far away, while Cecile is a wealthy lawyer living nearby. When the parents need visits and financial aid, Cecile has an obligation to bear a higher proportion of these burdens than her sister. This results from her abilities, rather than from the quantities of sacrifice made by the parents earlier.

"Sacrifices have an important causal role in creating an ongoing friendship, which may lead us to assume incorrectly that it is the sacrifices that are the source of the obligation. That the source is the friendship instead can be seen by examining cases in which the sacrifices occurred but the friendship, for some reason, did not develop or persist. For example, if a woman gives up her newborn child for adoption, and if no feelings of love ever develop on either side, it seems that the grown child does not have an obligation to 'repay' her for her sacrifices in pregnancy. For that matter, if the adopted child has an unimpaired love relationship with the adoptive parents, he or she has the same obligations to help them as a natural child would have."

Jane English, "What Do Grown Children Owe Their Parents?" in *Morality and Moral Controversies*, ed. John Arthur (Englewood Cliffs, 1981), pp. 150–51.

APPENDIX B

Value-Balancing

The table below, drawn up in 1970 for and against American withdrawal from Vietnam and concluding in favor, illustrates the type of value-balancing recommended in chapter 5. Useful in many contexts, personal as well as social, such value tables are especially desirable when issues are important and deserve careful consideration. Plus and minus numbers, for values and disvalues, allow surer calculation. The more complex the issue and the closer the verdict, the more helpful the numbers become.

Values and Disvalues	Weighting (for and against)	Number
1. More even distribution of wealth in Cambodia, Laos, and South Vietnam	Neither so considerable nor so sure an effect as to weigh very heavily (for)	1
2. Mass purge in Cambodia, Laos, and South Vietnam	Very likely and probably considerable, so weighs more heavily (against)	−2
3. End of destruction, demoralization of war in these three countries	Both certain and important: still more important than the preceding negative consideration (for)	3
4. Elimination of escalation risk	The elimination certain but the risk small, so this weighs no heavier than 1 (for)	1
5. More irenic international climate, with lessened risk of world war	Also certain, but slight, so same weight (for)	1

186 Value-Balancing

6. Long-lasting communistic police state in Cambodia, Laos, and South Vietnam	The high likelihood and the high priority of the values affected give this great weight (against)	−4
7. Greatly increased funds for foreign aid, with probable use of a fraction	Less important than 3, more important than 1 or 4 (for)	2
8. Greatly decreased unrest in U.S.	Since the unrest not great and the decrease not total, same low weight as for 1 and 4 (for)	1
9. Greater funds, attention for internal problems of U.S.	Since likelihood of internal use greater than for 7, but problems less urgent, same value as for 7 (for)	2
10. Uncertain risk for Burma, Thailand, and Malaysia	The stakes fairly high; but the uncertainty warrants a low rating	−1
	Total	4

Adapted from Garth Hallett, "Training in Practical Wisdom: the Decision Seminar," *Gregorianum* 52 (1971): 789–91. Though many of these estimates still look accurate, hindsight suggests some adjustments in the weighting.

Notes

Chapter 1: Moral Reasoning

1. Brian H. Smith, "Responsibilities Regarding Morally Questionable Policies," in *Personal Values in Public Policy*, ed. John C. Haughey (New York, 1979), p. 132.
2. Martin Gansberg, "38 Who Saw Murder Didn't Call Police," in *Exploring Philosophy*, ed. Peter A. French (Cambridge, Mass., 1970), p. 5; reprinted from *The New York Times* (Friday, March 27, 1964).
3. Ibid.
4. Quoted from the Springfield *Monitor* in Frank C. Sharp, *Ethics* (New York, 1928), p. 75.
5. William James, *Talks to Teachers on Psychology* (New York, 1939), pp. 65–66.
6. Charles Darwin, *Autobiography and Selected Letters*, ed. F. Darwin (New York, 1958), pp. 53–54.

Chapter 2: Are Answers Possible?

1. Quoted in Robert Baum, *Ethical Arguments for Analysis*, brief edition (New York, 1975), p. 59.
2. Bertrand Russell, *Philosophical Essays* (New York, 1966), p. 20.
3. Ruth Benedict, "An Anthropologist's View of Values and Morality," in *The Problems of Philosophy*, 2d ed., ed. W. Alston and R. Brandt (Boston, 1974), p. 133.
4. Renford Bambrough, "A Proof of the Objectivity of Morals," in *Situationism and the New Morality*, ed. R. Cunningham (New York, 1970), p. 110.
5. Benedict, "An Anthropologist's View," p. 133.

6. David Hume, *An Enquiry concerning the Principles of Morals*, Appendix I, 240.
7. Bambrough, "Proof," p. 114.
8. Jean-Paul Sartre, *Existentialism*, trans. B. Frechtman (New York, 1947), pp. 28-30.
9. James Boswell, *Boswell's Life of Johnson*, ed. G. B. Hill, rev. L. F. Powell, 6 vols. (Oxford, 1934), vol. 2, p. 22.

Chapter 3: Sound Moral Arguments

1. *Family Week*, September 19, 1971.

Chapter 4: Analysis and Charity

1. Milton Friedman, "The Social Responsibility of Business Is to Increase Its Profits," *The New York Times Magazine*, September 13, 1970, p. 33.

Chapter 6: Universal Norms

1. Basil Mitchell, "Ideals, Roles, and Rules," in *Norm and Context in Christian Ethics*, ed. G. Outka and P. Ramsey (New York, 1968), p. 359.

Chapter 7: Rules of Preference

1. John Stuart Mill, *Utilitarianism*, chapter 2.
2. Saint Basil, *Concerning Baptism*, in *Ascetical Works*, trans. M. Wagner (New York, 1950), p. 428.
3. Martin Luther, *The Freedom of a Christian*, in *Martin Luther: Selections from His Writings*, ed. J. Dillenberger (Chicago, 1961), p. 73.
4. A. C. Ewing, *Ethics* (New York, 1953), p. 38.
5. Ibid.

Chapter 8: Morality and Law

1. John Stuart Mill, *On Liberty*, in Great Books of the Western World, ed. Robert M. Hutchins, vol. 43 (Chicago, 1952), p. 271.

2. Basil Mitchell, *Law, Morality, and Religion in a Secular Society* (London, 1970), p. 135.

3. Translation by G. M. A. Grube, in *The Trial and Death of Socrates* (Indianapolis, 1975).